THE SAVE AND PROSPER
Book of Money

Edited by Margaret Allen

COLLINS: LONDON AND GLASGOW

© Dale Publications Ltd 1971

Published by Wm Collins Sons & Co Ltd
Collins Clear-Type Press, Glasgow

ISBN 0 00 412001 9

Printed and bound in Great Britain by
Hazell Watson and Viney Ltd, Aylesbury, Bucks

THE SAVE AND PROSPER
Book of Money

Created and produced by
Dale Publications Ltd
12 Duke Street, St James's
London SW1

Designed by Hardy/Escasany

*Contributors
include:*
Susan Bevan
Halldora Blair
Pamela Buonaventura
Walter B. Deadman
Derek Forbes
John Gaselee
William Halden
Ronald Irving
Ian Morison
Danny O'Shea
Nicolas Travers
Geoffrey Van Dyke

Contents

trust funds; banks; owners; finance companies
– how much to borrow – caution – costs – conditions – qualifications for borrowing – types of
houses – the amount of the loan – special cases –
building and repairs – kinds of mortgages – tax
relief – mortgage guarantees – mortgage protection – standing mortgages – joint income
mortgages – escalator mortgages – endowment
mortgages – with profit endowment mortgages –
decreasing endowment – option mortgages –
endowment option mortgages – 100% mortgage
– savings schemes – missing payments – the ideal
borrower.

Protecting your home and possessions – values –
insuring your possessions – cover and cost –
restrictions – "all-risks" insurance – how to
insure – "agreed values" – insuring clothes –
making a claim – liability – body and limb insurance – non-cancellable insurance – other
insurances.

Protection and investment – main types –
annuities – saving – where to get life assurance –
insurance companies – agents – brokers – kinds
of policy – whole life policies – endowment –
how much to cover – costs – tax relief – unit-linked assurance – selection – tax – property
bonds – for and against – selection.

Looking after your retirement – state pensions –
flat rate pensions – state graduated – supplementary benefits – what to expect – when you
receive state pensions – private pension schemes
– legal aspects – calculation of company
pensions – capital sums at retirement – employers' contributions – tax angle – ages – changing
jobs – transferable schemes – widows' pensions
– guarantees from employers – avoiding estate
duty – increases in pensions after retirement –
associated employee benefits – lump sums to
families – long-term disability schemes –
women's pension rights – discrimination – finding your own pension scheme – specialist
advice.

Real costs – what kind of car – new or second-hand – how to buy a car – driving away – depreciation – standing charges – garaging – price of
petrol, repairs, servicing – saving money.

actions – interest on judgements – rights to claim interest on a debt or damages for injury – protection for investors – bankruptcy – the Official Receiver – lending – solicitors and estate agents – house buying or selling – solicitors' charges – cheques – hire purchase and credit agreements – second hand cars – defective goods – cancelling agreements – shopping – guarantees – misleading descriptions – money-lenders – settlements and trusts – infants and money – references – law in Scotland and Northern Ireland.

Index

Introduction

Welcome to the first edition of the Save & Prosper *Book of Money*. It has been designed to help the average man, woman or family to use their money to the best advantage. Many people do not spend or save their own money as efficiently as they could, and very rarely have more than the vaguest understanding of the sources of money, other than their wages or salary, which may be available to them. The *Book of Money* has not been written for the specialist. What we have tried to explain – in as simple terms as possible – are the basic facts of money as related to the average man or woman. Wherever possible, the book has been written in straightforward everyday language avoiding financial "jargon". Where a technical term has been unavoidable we have explained it.

This book will not tell you *all* about money; that is not its purpose. Lengthy and technical books have been written on almost every topic covered here, and when you have read or used this book you may wish to go on to more detailed and complicated works on the various facets of finance. But for Mr., Miss or Mrs. Average, the *Book of Money* should answer their major queries on saving, borrowing, buying a house or car, making a will, taxation and a host of other subjects.

You can start at chapter 1 and work your way through the book, if you are a beginner. Each subject leads naturally to the next and the sequence chosen is that which we believe the average person would take in his or her financial affairs. A warning: interest rates, tax rules, mortgage arrangements, laws, pension arrangements etc. can change and are subject to adjustment all the time. Before you act on anything you may read in the book check that there have been no changes in any aspect. The facts and figures in this book are those which applied to the best of our knowledge in June, 1971.

Chapter I

Putting your money to work

Money is a fascinating subject to most of us whether we have any or not. Many people often have far more money than they realise – they simply do not use their available cash, savings, wages or salary properly. Even those who can point proudly to their savings are not always getting the most out of them that they could, and certainly few people realise exactly what it costs them to borrow, whether it is from a bank, a building society, or on a hire purchase transaction. And as far as tax goes, if everyone claimed the allowance to which they may be entitled, the Government might be forced to put the rates up to get in the same amount it collects from us today.

For most people the main source of their money is their wages or salary. This book does not discuss these. What it will tell you is how to use the wages and salary you may get. Using money involves:

The sources of money

- Saving
- Borrowing
- Spending

The idea of putting money to work is relatively new. Until very recently the ordinary person found it difficult enough to survive on his or her earnings, let alone think about savings, pension schemes, buying cars or insurance. If they could, money was put away for a "rainy day", more often than not, under the bed, rather than in the bank. A mortgage on a house was about as far as most people felt they could go.

Two things have changed all that completely:

The majority of people no longer live at the survival level: we are all better off. They may not wish to save, buy a house, or a car, but the vast majority could save if they wished to; and many more who think they can't, also could if they used their money more sensibly.

Inflation – a technical word for something we all know about – the £1 today buys less than it did last year, and even less than the year before that. A glance at the graph opposite shows you just what has happened. It shows you how much you would need today to buy what you could get with £1 in 1950. Money is only as valuable as what it will buy.

£2.05
£2.00
£1.75
£1.50
£1.25
£1.00

1950 '55 '60 '65 '70

How prices have risen over the last 20 years.

 Look closely at your money to make sure you are using it efficiently and remember that in the face of inflation your money must earn its keep.

Savings

Chapter two deals with savings in detail. It is designed to help those who may only have a small amount to save, as well as people with substantial capital. Money should not be saved in a box at home. Even if it isn't actually stolen, inflation will gradually eat it away. So you must put your savings to work for you to offset this. They can do this in two ways:

● *Earn an income.* This means that you get paid a fixed amount from some organisation or other for leaving your money with them for some time. We call this *interest*, and it is usually expressed as a percentage (or p.c. or %). For example, 5% means that you will get £5 a year for every £100 you save.

● *Make a capital gain.* Quite simply this means paying a certain sum for something you buy which you sell later at a higher price. For example: you may buy something which becomes rare; or you may have paid less than it was really worth; or again inflation may put prices up. If long-term gain is your primary purpose, Chapter 5 on house buying, 8 on life assurance, 9 on pensions, 12 on the stock exchange, 13 on unit trusts, 14 on antiques and similar objects, will all help you.

Money can earn interest and make a capital gain at the same time. Read chapters 12 and 13.

A warning

If you go for gain, you run the chance of a loss, so know what you are doing.

Starting to save

This book will tell you a lot of useful things, but not, unfortunately, how to make yourself save. Still, there are some ways you can help yourself to start the habit. They may sound obvious, but are worth repeating.

Try to enjoy saving

Scrooge found saving easy because he liked it better than spending. While no-one wants to go quite as far as he did, we can at least make saving a bit more pleasant for ourselves by having a definite, enjoyable end in view. Don't just put aside money vaguely for a "rainy day" or a "holiday sometime". Work out the object in detail. Encourage yourself with the travel brochures, and books about the Greek Islands you intend to visit or by turning yourself into an expert on the Aston Martin, even if you have no hope of getting it for years.

Nothing is more difficult than just vaguely "trying to save". Make the effort to sit down and work out exactly how much you can put aside each month and stick to it. This is easier if the way you decide to save does not involve you in any extra inconvenience such as paying a special visit to some bank or office to deposit the money, or sending it off in the post. Anything like that can shake your resolve. So fit your saving into your routine. Best of all, have an arrangement which makes it an effort not to save rather than the other way around. If you have a current account at the bank, have a standing order which automatically transfers what you want to save to the right place. Or join the Save As You Earn scheme – a rewarding thing to do anyway as you will see on page 29, then you can have your savings deducted from your pay packet by your employer.

Get into a savings routine

Before going on to the following chapters, three questions must be answered:

1) How long can or are you prepared to commit your savings without wanting to withdraw them?
   The shorter the time you are prepared to leave your savings, or the more often you are going to want to withdraw some of them, then the more of an administrative nuisance you become to whichever body has the use of them. Correspondingly, they will pay you a better income on your money if you are prepared to commit them for a long period.

The longer notice you can give for withdrawing your savings the more you can earn from them.

WISEGUIDE

---

2) Are you prepared to take a risk?
   Savings on which you are prepared to take a risk will obviously have a chance of earning more than savings which you cannot afford to lose. For one thing, they are probably in the market for capital gains – but remember that a capital gain may turn into a capital loss.

Risk means greater opportunity to gain and greater chance to lose.

WISEGUIDE

---

3) Do you want your savings to earn money for you to spend now or to build up for the future?
   If your savings are earning income you can often choose

whether to spend that income when it is paid to you (usually at least once a year) or to plough it back into more savings. Some of the savings mechanisms we shall be describing pay no annual income at all but automatically plough it back. Remember that if you spend the income as it arises, your savings cannot grow and so have no chance of keeping up with inflation.

WISEGUIDE

You can't have your cake and eat it.

Before you go on to chapter 2, study which category your savings come into.

Category 1 Money you have in the background for emergencies or bills which you probably dip into every so often for a "luxury" purchase.

Category 2 Money you will need for use in a relatively short time ahead – say within five years.
Examples: Saving to get married; saving for a car; saving for your annual holiday or for Christmas.

Category 3 Savings which are earmarked for use some time in the future.
Examples: Saving up for retirement; for a "once in a lifetime holiday"; planning ahead for your children's education.

Category 4 Money which is not positively earmarked for anything and which you are prepared to risk.

For:
Savings in Categories 1 & 2 – chapter 2, section A.

Savings in Category 3 — chapter 2, section B and chapters 8, 9, 12, 13.

Savings in Category 4 — chapter 2, but also 12, 13 and 14.

A point to watch ● Tax considerations. Make sure your savings make the most of your tax position. Some savings are tax-free, others tax-paid, others taxable. Read chapters 2, 12, 13 and 16, which cover all aspects of personal taxation.

Borrowing Using other people's money for your own benefit has never been regarded as quite as respectable as saving. Yet most people who frown on borrowing often do it themselves on quite a large scale in relation to their total available funds. It is not often realised that you can get the best of all possible worlds by saving and borrowing at the same time. The most striking example of this,

of course, is when people buy a house – read chapters 5 & 6 carefully. Very few people today pay cash for a house regardless of their financial position. They know that there are ways of extending their payment over many years and saving tax at the same time. Very sensibly, if they have spare cash available, they make it earn them an income rather than being locked up in a solid asset like a house. Remember that you borrow from other people's savings – you should consider *making* yourself borrow.

Yet if you look closely at borrowing you will see that it has a much longer history than saving which is a relatively new idea. People were busy borrowing in ancient Greece and the British themselves started over 600 years ago.

How HP grew up

The use of instalment credit or hire purchase as most people call it, where the buyer repays an agreed amount in regular instalments, is well over 300 years old.

First it was mainly used in connection with pianos and sewing machines. Originally the manufacturer or seller provided the finance, but eventually specialist hire purchase finance companies came into existence and they dominate the market today.

WISEGUIDE

Remember that there is nothing wrong with borrowing provided that you don't go beyond your means.

Points to watch

● Getting credit or borrowing from a company or a bank will cost you money. This can vary enormously so "shop around" if you can.

● Read chapter 3 which explains in detail all the advantages and disadvantages in borrowing.

● Know what protection you can get – see chapter 3, and chapter 17 on the law.

Spending

This book will not tell you where to buy the cheapest meat or groceries, or the best value in refrigerators or any household purchases of that type, but it will help you in getting the best value in major purchases, outside the normal running of the home, which eventually affect most families and individuals.

This type of spending is not always on a tangible product. It may be on a service, like protecting your home and its contents, or your car against damage or theft. It may be spending now on something like life assurance (chapter 8), or in a pension scheme (chapter 9), which will eventually make your own old age more comfortable, or provide some guaranteed security for your dependents. It may also mean avoiding unnecessary spending, like paying too much for a house (chapter 5) or car (chapter 10), or more tax than you need simply because you do not know all the allowances you can claim (chapter 16).

These are some of the kinds of spending dealt with in this book. You must apply the same principles as you would when borrowing or saving:

1. How much can you afford?
2. Can you afford to take a risk?
3. Do you want the benefits now or later?

WISEGUIDE

Running an individual or a family budget is a complicated affair. Know what you are doing and sort out your priorities.

Ask yourself some of the following questions:

● Have you covered your normal living expenses? If you have then –

● Could you cut these by more sensible budgeting? For example would it be better to buy rather than rent your house or flat?

● Are you properly insured? Are your dependants protected?

● Have you joined a company pension scheme if you are eligible for one?
If you are self employed have you taken out a private pension scheme?

● Do you really need a car? And if you do, do you know what it *really* costs to run? Have you got the right sort of insurance?

● Can you afford to put some money in shares on the Stock Exchange or in Unit Trusts? Do you know the risks involved? Do you know how to buy them? Do you know exactly what you are buying when you buy a share or unit trust?

● Do you know what tax is all about? Can you fill in a tax return? Do you know the allowances to which you may be entitled?

● Have you made a will? Everyone should, even if they think they have little to leave.

● Do you know all the legal aspects of saving, borrowing, lending and gambling money?

WISEGUIDE

Unless you can answer all these questions, the *Book of Money* could be extremely useful for you in making your money earn more money for you and avoiding loss. Money doesn't grow on trees, but carefully managed it can grow and provide you with a nest egg just at the time you most need it.

Saving without risk

The last chapter posed a number of questions to be answered by the saver who wants to put his money to work. The most important of these was: Can I afford to take a risk?

If your answer to this question was NO, then this is the chapter to find the ways of money-making saving which are open to you.

If you answered YES – do not ignore this chapter. Although you will be going on to the exciting fields which open out later in the book, you will still find a lot to interest you here.

Before going any further you have another important question to answer:

How long can I commit my money without wanting to claim it back?

Think carefully about the answer to this one. You may think that you can leave your money for a long period, but make sure that first you have enough cash to meet any emergency which may crop up.

This chapter is divided into two parts according to the answer you give.

SECTION A deals with ways you can save money which you know you're going to need within four or five years, or think you may need.

SECTION B is for money you know you can commit for four or five years or more. In some cases you will just not be allowed to withdraw your money at short notice. In other cases you will lose out on income if you do.

Note: • Although we have taken five years as the dividing line, almost all the ways of saving described in Section A in fact allow you to withdraw your money without penalty in a month or less.

• There are ways of saving in Section B where a commitment of less than four years may be possible.
And as the years go by the penalties for withdrawing your money too soon tend to get less and less. So if you want to save for, say, three years, Section B may offer opportunities to you.

• Even if you can commit your money for five years or longer, you may well find some Section A methods attractive.

SECTION A: SHORT-TERM SAVING

Many of the ways of saving described in this chapter are part of the National Savings movement. This includes the National Savings Bank (formerly the Post Office Savings Bank), Savings Certificates, Premium Bonds, British Savings Bonds, the Trustee

Can I afford to take a risk?

How long can I commit my money without wanting to claim it back?

The National Savings Bank

Savings Banks, and the Save-As-You-Earn scheme. In all these cases, the Government *guarantees* the *safety* of both the *money* deposited and the *interest* promised.

This copper-bottomed security was the great advantage of the National Savings Bank when it started back in the last century. Then privately-run financial institutions frequently failed, and many people lost their money in bank crashes and so on. Nowadays, when the banks, building societies and the like offer pretty well water-tight security themselves, the Government guarantees are less significant.

However, official backing brings another advantage. Because the Government is keen to encourage saving, it offers tax concessions on some forms of National Savings. In this instance, the inducement is the allowance of the first £21 of yearly interest on an ordinary account free from tax. This is the interest on £600 in the N.S.B.

As you will see from the table, 3·5% tax-free is equal to nearly 6% on which tax must be paid.

An important point to remember: Although the National Savings Bank is called a bank, it does not offer all the various services which we have come to expect from the commercial banks. It will not arrange foreign currency for your overseas holidays, let you have an overdraft or loan, or allow you to pay over money from your account with a cheque. The one service it does offer is the making of regular payments from your account for bills and so on, as long as these are not more frequent than once a month. A small charge is made for this.

● Ordinary Account

● Investment Account

The Ordinary account (which offers 3·5% at present) is designed for people who want to be able to withdraw their savings on demand. The Investment account (7·5%) offers a higher rate of interest in exchange for requiring one month's notice before you withdraw your money.

How it works

**National Savings Bank
Ordinary Account**

Interest
3.5% (equivalent to 5.7% on which income tax has to be paid)
Minimum Investment
£0.25
Maximum Investment
£10,000
Withdrawal Terms
£20 on demand and the remainder at 3 or 4 days notice
Tax points
Interest on the first £600 invested is free of tax for all but surtax payers

● You can open both types of account over the counter at any post office branch. When you make your first deposit you will be issued with a bank book which records all your transactions – payments and withdrawals. This will have to be filled in every time you make a transaction so be sure you have your bank book with you when you go to the Post Office.

● The bank book has to be returned to the Post Office headquarters every time two pages are completed. This can take several days, so you won't want to make too many small transactions.

● Your money starts earning interest from the first day of the month after the deposit is made, and goes on earning it until the first day of the month in which you take the money out of your account. So it pays to be organised about your payments and withdrawals. If you pay in the money on the first of the month it will earn interest during that month, but if you delay for a few days you will not earn any income until the next month.

● When you want to withdraw money from your ordinary account, up to £20 can be withdrawn on demand from any branch of the Post Office on any day. If you want more than this, you will have to apply in writing or pay for a telegram to be sent to headquarters. If you withdraw more than £5 twice in any week, your bank book will have to go back to head office for checking.

● If you want to withdraw money from your investment account, you must give one month's notice and send in a written application.

For

The great advantage of the National Savings Bank is its convenience. The 21,000 or so branches at Post Offices around the country mean that no-one has to go far out of his way to use his account. And branches are open during normal shopping and office hours, which is not true of the commercial banks.

This, plus the fact that your money can be withdrawn on demand, means that some people prefer to keep the money for their day-to-day requirements in the National Savings Bank, rather than having a current account at a commercial bank. Also there are no bank charges.

This is only a good idea, though, if the amounts you are dealing with from day to day are fairly small. Remember that the most you can take out in a week is £20, and you will periodically be without access to your money for several days while your book is being checked. Young people in their first jobs, for example, might use a National Savings Bank account in this way. It is also a very good way for children to learn to manage their money.

Remember – if you are using your account as a current account you will not earn much interest on it.

Your National Savings Bank account is particularly suitable for your "emergency fund" – that sum of money you put aside regularly to meet the unexpected crises and bills. The bank itself will deal with regular payments.

Remember to be organised about your payments and withdrawals so as not to lose income unnecessarily.

Against

The interest rate does not compare well with other alternatives. So this is not the place for savings you are putting aside for a longer-term objective – even if this is only six months or so ahead.

Remember – if you do not pay tax on your interest, the tax concession means nothing to you.

When it comes to your day-to-day money, the N.S.B. has a big disadvantage compared with a commercial bank current account, and also with an ordinary account with the Trustee Savings Bank (see chapter 4). IT DOES NOT ALLOW PAYMENT BY CHEQUE. Nor does it offer other banking services. So if your financial affairs need this kind of service, the N.S.B. is not for you.

The National Savings Bank ordinary account

Is it for me? Should I save in a National Savings Bank ordinary account?

- is not for saving for your nest egg

- is good for your "emergency fund" for bills and crises

- may be used as a current account when smaller sums are involved, but does not provide other banking services

- is a good way to save for short periods.

WISEGUIDE

Remember that if you can commit your money for a longer period you can get better rates of interest elsewhere; for instance, it is worth looking at the building societies, too.

The National Savings Bank investment account

National Savings Bank Investment Account

Interest
7.5%
Minimum Investment
£1
Maximum Investment
£10,000
Withdrawal Terms
1 month's notice

The interest rate here compares well with other methods of saving described in Section A. Notice, though, that the rate can rise and fall from time to time.

The interest is particularly attractive if you are not liable to any income tax on your interest, because the very good rates paid by the building societies will be less attractive to you. At the current rates, the N.S.B. investment account also has a slight edge over the basically similar Trustee Savings Bank Investment Account.

WISEGUIDE

Whatever your savings requirements are, you will have to have £50 earning a lower rate of interest in the National Savings Bank ordinary account before you can have an investment account as well.

The Trustee Savings Bank

The Trustee Savings Banks are most easily described as a cross between the commercial banks and the National Savings Banks.

Their operations are non-profit making, and subject to government supervision.

The facilities these banks offer the saver are pretty well identical to those of the National Savings Banks, and they are part of the National Savings movement. It is also possible to open a T.S.B. cheque account comparable to a commercial bank current account on which no interest is paid.

However, the T.S.Bs also offer many of the services of a commercial bank. You can, for instance, pay by cheque from your T.S.B. account first acquiring the cheque from the T.S.B. office, and they will arrange your travellers' cheques and foreign currency. They do not, at the moment, offer overdrafts and loans.

The Trustee banks are organised on a local basis, and the Manchester Trustee Savings Bank is, for example, quite independent of the London T.S.B. But they are all governed by the same rules and offer the same services, so from the saver's point of view they are all very much the same.

How it works

The rules for using a Trustee Savings Bank Ordinary account are very similar to those applying to the comparable account with the National Savings Bank.

The most important difference is that withdrawing money on demand is much easier from a T.S.B. ordinary account than from an ordinary account with the National Savings Bank, since £100 can be withdrawn on demand.

For

The important consideration here is whether the T.S.B. ordinary account offers better facilities for keeping your ready money and your "emergency fund" than the similar account at the National Savings Bank. It is clear that the Trustee Banks have two important advantages. They offer a wider range of banking facilities and they allow you to withdraw far more of your money on demand.

Against

On the other hand, the T.S.Bs have far fewer branches than the National Savings Bank whose outlets are the post offices. This means that you will find a Trustee Savings Bank less useful if you do not happen to have one convenient to your office or home.

The rate of interest offered is again, not attractive to those who are putting their money away for any length of time.

A Trustee Savings Bank ordinary account

- is not for saving for your "nest egg"

- is a good place for money you may need at short notice

- has useful "extras" in the form of banking services

Is it for me? Should I save in a Trustee Savings Bank ordinary account?

This type of saving account offers all the advantages of a similar account with the National Savings Bank (see page 19) and the wider range of services which the T.S.Bs provide are an added inducement. You can, for example, have a cheque book in some cases.

A disincentive at the moment is the gap between the interest rates offered on the T.S.B. and N.S.B. accounts, for those not prepared to commit their money for as long as three months.

A similar account with the National Savings Bank is a better bet for most people at the moment.

WISEGUIDE

The commercial banks are described in detail in Chapter 4 where you can find details of the services they offer and the uses of a current account. We briefly mention there that the banks also offer facilities to savers who want to deposit their money for a period of time and earn interest on it. These are described here.

The Commercial Banks

- A Deposit or Savings account may be opened at any commercial bank branch. It need not necessarily be the same branch

How it works

Commercial Bank Deposit Account

Interest
2% below Bank Rate
(4% currently)
Minimum Investment
No limit
Maximum Investment
No limit
Withdrawal Terms
7 days notice

Commercial Bank Savings Account

Interest
4½% on first £250 invested
Deposit Account rate
thereafter
Minimum Investment
No limit
Maximum Investment
No limit
Withdrawal Terms
£20 On demand. Remainder at
7 days notice

at which you hold your current account, nor do you need to hold a current account at all if you do not want to.

● You will not usually get a special bank book for your deposit account. It is more common these days for account holders to keep track of their transactions through a bank statement which can be asked for as regularly as you want. In some cases, however, a bank book is issued. Savings account holders have a bank book used in the same way as a N.S.B. book.

● The difference between the two sorts of account is that the Savings account pays 4½% on the first £250 invested, and allows for easier withdrawal facilities. At the current level of bank rate (6%), this is higher than is deposit account rate, but this is not, of course, always the case.

● The interest on both accounts is paid on a daily basis over the whole period during which the money is deposited.

● You can withdraw money from your account only at the branch where the account is held. From a Savings account £20 may be drawn on demand and the remainder on a week's notice. If you have a Deposit account then you must give a week's notice before withdrawing any money.

For If you have a deposit account you will almost certainly have a current account as well. In that case you can arrange to save in your deposit account easily and painlessly by arranging for a regular transfer from your current account (on the day after pay day, perhaps).

The short notice required for withdrawals means that this is another place where you can put aside your "emergency fund" for crises and bills, and earn a bit of interest on it at the same time. Since the interest here is paid over the whole period of the deposit, your chances of getting some interest on money left for only a short time is greater than if you used an ordinary account with the National Savings or Trustee Savings banks for this purpose.

Against At the current level of bank rate (6%) the interest does not compare well with other forms of saving in either Sections A or B. So a deposit account is not the place to save up for a long-term objective, even if the objective is in the fairly near future (like your summer holiday).

A week's notice must be given before you can withdraw your money, so a deposit account will not suit you if you want immediate access to your savings. The fact that withdrawals can only be made from the one bank branch at which you have your account also makes your money that much less accessible.

A Commercial Bank Deposit account

● is another place to keep your emergency fund
● transfers from current account make saving simple
● it's not for saving for your "nest egg" because of the relatively low current interest rates, but this can change.

Is it for me? Should I save in a Commercial Bank deposit account?

Building societies are non-profitmaking organisations which offer a very convenient way of saving with very attractive interest rates at the moment.

In chapter 6 you can read about one side of their business – the ways in which they lend money to house purchasers. This money comes from the savings of their depositors.

The interest which the societies charge to borrowers and pay to lenders varies according to the ease with which savings can be attracted. At the moment the rates are as high as they have ever been.

Since their beginnings in the eighteenth century the building societies have enjoyed booming growth. There are now some 550 in all, with over 2000 branches between them. The giants of the business are the Halifax, the Abbey National and the Nationwide, all with over 150 branches.

Building Societies

The standard of security the societies offer these days is almost absolute. Societies have been known to fail, but not since their law was tightened up by the Building Societies' Act of 1960.

Still, why take even the slightest risk? There are two ways you can check whether your society is absolutely sound. One way is to deal only with those which have "Trustee Status". This means that they measure up to government standards. Alternatively, look for members of the Building Societies Association. Its members include about two-thirds of all the societies, its rules are strict, and it has considerable authority.

Security

Deposit and Share Accounts

These two vary very little in practice. You can also open a building society subscription share account which earns a bonus of $\frac{1}{2}\%$ or more to the regular saver. Although the savings period often appears long – 4 or 7 years is common – you can, in practice, withdraw at any time and the bonus holds good until you stop saving.

● Both types of account can be opened at any building society branch, which can be found in any High Street. Alternatively, you can open an account by filling in an application and sending it through the post.

Is it for me? Should I save in a building society account?

● If you have an account with one Society you can deal with any of its branches, but not, of course, with the branches of any other society, unless you have an account there too.

● The interest paid on share accounts is slightly higher than that on deposit accounts, because technically share account holders are carrying slightly more risk. In the event of the society's winding up, deposit account holders have first claim on its assets. Share account holders are not shareholders in the usual sense of the word since the building societies are non profit-making, but they do have the right to attend and vote at the society's annual general meeting – not an especially exciting privilege.

Saving without risk

5%-5.25% (equivalent to
8.2%-8.6%
on which tax has to be paid)
Minimum Investment.
I share
Maximum Investment
£10,000 in any one society
Withdrawal Terms
Vary. Normally £100 on
demand (up to £500 sometimes
allowed by larger societies).
Remainder at a few days notice
Tax Points
Interest is paid net of income
tax. It must be grossed up by
standard rate of tax for
assessment of surtax

● When you open an account you receive a pass book which is used in the same way as a National Savings Bank book.

● Building society interest is earned on a daily basis. It starts the first day after you invest the money, and continues over the whole period during which your money is with the society.

● Building society interest is paid net of tax. The tax is paid by the society at a special low rate. This means that for income tax payers, the rates quoted by building societies are the equivalent of much larger amounts on which tax would have to be paid.

Take a look at the table. The current 5% offered on a share account is the equivalent of 8·2% on which tax has to be paid. If you do not pay tax you cannot reclaim anything. All you are interested in is the quoted rate.

● Problems for surtax payers: for surtax purposes, income is grossed up at the standard rate of tax. So, for example, although you may only have received 5% on your building society account, you will have to pay surtax on 8·2%.

WISEGUIDE

Since the chances of your building society failing are now so remote, there is no good reason for forgoing the slightly better rates of interest available from a share account.

For The current rates of interest quoted net represent the best return available to the income tax payer without committing savings for several years.

Easy withdrawal terms are also a bonus to those who want to use their account for their day-to-day financial needs, and the method of interest payment means that money saved for only a short time has a better chance of earning interest than in the National Savings Bank.

Savers with the building society usually get special consideration when applying to their society for a mortgage. This makes the building society an especially good place for young people to save.

Against Because interest is paid net of tax and this cannot be reclaimed, the rate offered is not attractive to people who are not liable to tax. Surtax payers will probably also find other forms of saving more suitable.

Even the biggest building society cannot compare with the National Savings Bank in terms of branches, so unless you have a branch very handy to your home or office you will have to be organised about your building society savings. The same goes for your day-to-day money needs if you are using your building society account for these. Of course, the bigger the society – in terms of numbers of branches – the better from this point of view.

The societies do not offer any of the banking services offered by commercial and trustee savings banks – in particular there are no facilities for paying out from your account by cheque. You will probably do better to keep your current account elsewhere, if you are not managing to save anything out of it.

A building society account

- is a very rewarding way to save at current rates of interest
- is good, too, for your emergency fund for bills and unexpected outgoings
- is less good for your day-to-day money needs unless you have a convenient branch and do not require other banking services

Finance companies

Bridging the gap between our Group A and Group B savings method are the finance companies, which offer a variety of interest rates according to the length of time you are prepared to commit your savings. They are sometimes called H.P. companies, sometimes finance houses, and sometimes even Industrial Banks. You normally come across them through their advertisements in the newspapers.

How it works

Like the building societies, the finance companies' business is borrowing from savers on the one hand and lending out at interest on the other. But there are important differences. Building societies lend exclusively to house purchasers so that in cases of default they are usually left with a valuable asset – the house. Finance houses, on the other hand, lend to purchasers of all manner of things, most of which will deteriorate between the time of the loan and the time of a possible default.

Their most important business is car hire purchase, but they also lend to people buying expensive items of household equipment, and to industrial concerns for plant, vehicles and machinery.

Finance company business is, consequently, more risky than that of the building societies. This is the more true because, unlike building societies, they are profit-making concerns, and therefore more likely to countenance risk in the interest of business. So, before saving your money with a finance company, assure yourself of the reputation of the undertaking.

Most companies are absolutely reliable, but some notable failures have occurred in this line of business. Most of the commercial banks own or have an interest in a finance company, and you can feel absolutely safe about putting your savings with these; but otherwise, give this way of saving a miss unless you can understand the company's balance sheet or have someone to go to for advice.

Is it for me? Should I save with a finance company?

The terms on which you can put your money with a finance company vary considerably between one concern and another.

- There is no standard rate of interest, and this varies both with the length of time you are prepared to commit your money and with the risk involved.

● At the moment you can expect around 4% if you give seven days' notice of withdrawal, and 7·5% if you are prepared to wait for three months.

Remember: above average rates of interest probably mean above average risk.

● To find out the ways in which you can put your money with one of these companies, there is no alternative to writing away for further details to each separately. Study the terms carefully.

● But you can discuss with your bank manager and ask his advice on the terms offered by any company with which the bank is connected.

● Sometimes your bank branch will accept deposits for the finance companies with which it is connected, and this makes regular saving by this means a possibility. Otherwise, finance house investment is more appropriate to "lump sum" deposits.

● Unfortunately, some of the largest and best-known companies will accept only very large deposits of £5,000 or £10,000.

For The interest rates offered are attractive when a longer-term commitment can be made. So this might be the place for your medium-term saving towards an objective, say, a year or two ahead. Or if you have quite a large sum of money to save for a longer period, you will probably get still better terms.

Against If you want to have your money readily available then the finance companies have nothing to offer beyond that available from other forms of saving which offer greater convenience and overall reliability.

WISEGUIDE

Finance companies
● Interest rates can be attractive, but not for the unwary.

SECTION B: LONGER-TERM SAVING

We said at the beginning of this chapter that there is no firm dividing line between the forms of saving described in Section A and in Section B. But broadly speaking, this section will only interest you if you want to put your money away for four or five years or more. There are opportunities here for shorter-term saving, but in no case can money be withdrawn immediately without some penalty.

Savings certificates Savings certificates are another branch of the National Savings movement, this time for the longer-term saver. The government is particularly generous in its encouragement of saving by this means because the return on certificates is free of all tax.

There have been fifteen issues of certificates made since 1916. The latest, the Decimal Issue, is the only one now on sale.

Previous issues continue to exist and pay interest, though, and you might perhaps inherit them.

Each issue of certificates in the past has been made on slightly different terms, and the terms of the Decimal Issue are the best yet. We only deal with this issue here, but you can find out the details of the others from your local post office.

How it works

● Savings certificates do not pay interest as you go along in the usual way. Instead, when your certificates come to the end of their life, you get back your original investment plus 25%. So, if you bought £100 worth of certificates today, you would get back £125 in four years' time.

● The certificates themselves are documents stating that you have purchased a certain number of units. Each unit costs £1, and this is the smallest amount you can invest at a time.

● You can buy your certificates at post offices, and also from the commercial and trustee savings banks. When you make your first purchase of units, you will receive a registration number which is printed on all the certificates you hold, and a Holder's card which gives this number and the details of the certificates you own. Take care not to mislay your card, and particularly not to forget your number, because this must be given whenever you buy more certificates or cash them in.

● It is most important to notice that the interest on your certificates builds up with time, starting at low levels. In the normal course of events you will not be expected to receive any interest until four years are up, but if you do have to cash in your certificates, the interest is calculated as follows:

At the end of the first year: 3% (4·9% taxable equiv.)

At the end of the second year: 4·37% (7·1% t.e.)

At the end of the third year: 6·97% (11·4% t.e.)

At the end of the fourth year: 8·69% (14·2% t.e.)

This works out at the compound rate of 5·74% (9·4% taxable equivalent).

If you do have to cash in your certificates prematurely you will only receive the interest for the completed years. So try to avoid this if at all possible.

The Decimal Issue caused quite a stir when it was launched in 1970 because of the very high rate of interest it offers to tax

Savings Certificate
Decimal Issue

Interest
5.74% (equivalent to 9.4% on which income tax has to be paid)
Minimum Investment
£1
Maximum Investment
£1,000
Withdrawal Terms
Money can be withdrawn at 8 days notice but interest paid is considerably reduced if the certificates are cashed within their 4 year life
Tax Points
Interest free of all tax

payers. This was taken as an indication that the government expected rates everywhere to continue to be very high over the next few years – and that means the rate on your mortgage, and your bank overdraft as well as on your savings, so it is a mixed blessing.

**Is it for me?
Should I save in
savings certificates?**

For Apart from the Save-As-You-Earn scheme which encourages regular savings with still better rates, this is the best interest normally available to tax payers on risk-free investments. Large sums of money lent for considerable numbers of years to local authorities or finance companies could earn a better rate in exchange for much greater inconvenience.

Purchasing certificates is easy and can be done at a very large number of outlets. If you have to withdraw your money before the four-year life of the certificates is up then you can do so relatively easily, although losing out on income, of course.

Against There is one better alternative available to those who can commit themselves to saving a set amount every month for five years, and that is the Save-As-You-Earn scheme. So do consider this if you can.

Those with large amounts to save will have to consider other alternatives in addition to the certificates, since the maximum holding of certificates allowed is £1,000. Every member of your family can hold this amount though.

The penalties for cashing in your certificates before their life is up are severe, so this is not for you unless you can make a longish commitment of your money.

The tax concession is what really makes savings certificates attractive, so those not liable to tax should look elsewhere.

WISEGUIDE

An excellent interest rate if you can definitely commit your money for the required period.

British Savings Bonds

Interest
7% per year with a 3% bonus if bonds are held for a full 5 years = 0.6% per annum. The bonus is equivalent to an extra 1% per year on which tax has to be paid.
Minimum Investment
£5
Maximum Investment
£10,000
Withdrawal Terms
1 months notice but bonus is lost if withdrawal is made before 5 years are up.

British Savings Bonds are yet another arm of the National Savings movement. They are the successors to the National Development Bonds and Defence Bonds, which were much the same thing under another name.

There have been twenty-one issues of this sort of bond, all with differing terms. Only the most recent one – the 7% British Savings Bond-is now on sale. The others are still in existence, though, and paying interest, so you may inherit them.

The government's special savings incentive here is a tax-free bonus of 3%, paid at the end of the bond's five year life.

● Bonds can be bought at any branch of the post office in units of £5 each.

● Interest is paid every six months, and is liable to tax.

● At the end of the five-year life of the bonds you must fill in the encashment application form, again available at the post office, and you will receive £103 for every £100 you have saved. This is tax free.

● Then if you like you can start all over again with another lot of bonds.

● To cash in your bonds you must give a month's notice and fill in an application form. Remember – if you cash in the bonds before the end of their life you will not get the bonus.

● If you cash in within a six-month period you will sacrifice all the interest earned on them during that period. So watch out for this if you have to sell your bonds prematurely.

Is it for me? Should I save in British Savings Bonds?

For

If the bonds are held for the full five years the return is reasonably good for income tax payers, and still better for surtax payers, for whom the tax-free bonus can represent a considerable sum in taxable terms.

The maximum holding allowed, £10,000, is considerably more than your allowance of savings certificates, so those who have exhausted their allowance of certificates can switch into bonds.

Since you can buy your bonds at any post office branch, this is a relatively convenient way to save, although £5 a time might be too much for some.

Against

The interest, even with bonus, is less than other forms of saving, with easier withdrawal terms.

If the capital bonus is lost the interest is even less attractive.

Those not liable to tax do not benefit from the tax relief, although the return is still reasonably good for these savers. The penalties for premature withdrawal are quite severe.

WISEGUIDE

Have some uses for tax payers, and especially surtax payers, but offers little that cannot be matched elsewhere at current interest rates.

Save As You Earn

The Save-As-You-Earn scheme, SAYE, is the best government effort so far to encourage savings by a high return and tax incentives. The appeal is to the regular saver willing to put aside a set amount month by month.

How it works

● Under the scheme you contract to save a regular amount between £1 and £20 every month for five years. And you must keep to your contract.

● The return does not come as a regular interest payment but as a bonus at the end of the contract period. This bonus is equivalent to one year's savings. So if you are saving £5 per month, or £300 over five years, you will receive a bonus of £60. This is free

Save As You Earn

Interest
Equivalent to 7.2% per year
when the contract is for
5 years (equivalent to 11.42%
on which tax has to be paid)
Minimum Investment
£1 per month
Maximum Investment
£20 per month
Withdrawal Terms
Money can be withdrawn on 8
working days notice but
interest paid is severely
reduced if the contract is not
maintained for its 5 year life.

of all tax so is roughly equivalent to a return of 11·42% a year which is subject to tax.

● If the money is left for a further two years, although no further contributions are made, the bonus is doubled. This represents 12·10% of taxable interest per year.

● Payments can be made into SAYE in cash, by cheque, giro or bankers' order. Another new feature of the scheme allows contributions to be deducted straight from your pay by your employer. If payments are missed a limited extension is made to the life of the contract.

● The building societies run identical schemes.

● If savings are withdrawn before the end of the contract period, the bonus is forfeited. Instead a return is made equivalent to a low rate of interest.

● If savings are withdrawn before the end of the first year, no interest at all is paid.

● If the withdrawal is made in the following years a rate equivalent to 2½% per year tax free is paid. This is equal to 4·1% of taxable income.

● If payments stop but the savings already made are not withdrawn, a rate equivalent to 4·5% a year tax free is paid (equal to 7·2% taxable).

● If savings have to be withdrawn because of death a rate of 4·5% tax free is paid.

● Partial withdrawals are not permitted.

Is it for me? Should I save in the Save-As-You-Earn scheme?

For The return is excellent, particularly for surtax payers, for whom it can be colossal. Deductions direct from pay make this a particularly easy and painless way of saving.

Against Penalties for premature withdrawal are severe. No-one who feels there is any chance of having to call on this money at short notice should embark on a contract.

Lump sum investments cannot be made. The return is far less attractive to those not liable to tax, but still good.

Save As You Earn

● permits a relatively small amount to be saved on excellent terms.

● is only for regular savers and those who have no prospect of needing their savings at short notice.

Local authority loans

Local authorities like your borough or rural district council borrow money from the public to help pay for services like roads and schools, and take some of the burden for these off their ratepayers.

On any day you will find a number of local authorities advertising for loans in the newspapers. They are all entirely independent in this respect, and set what terms they like. A small, poor council will probably have to give better terms than a wealthy London borough.

But in all cases you can be sure that your money is safe with a local authority, since every loan raised has to have government approval, and is then guaranteed by the Public Works Loans Board.

● To find out the opportunities available in this field, you must keep your own look-out in the newspapers. (A typical advertisement for a mythical authority is illustrated opposite.) If an advertisement arouses your interest write in to the authority concerned for further details.

● The advertisement will normally tell you the two most important things you want to know – namely the interest rate offered and the length of time the loan is required. Currently the average interest is $7\frac{1}{2}\%$ for one year and 8% for 3–5 years, but these rates rise and fall considerably.

● You are not, of course, confined to lending to your own authority, but many people like to be involved in their community in this way. Also you may find that you can conduct the transaction over the counter at your town hall.

● A variety of different types of mortgages and bonds are used by authorities for fund raising. Some are quite simple, requiring only a certificate of registration, but others require a more complicated deed to be prepared.

● The period of the loan varies; the average is two to five years, but it is sometimes possible to lend for only a year.

● You should notice that premature withdrawal of your money will prove difficult, and will be severely penalised by charges.

This is a way of saving large sums absolutely safely at a good rate of interest. It should particularly interest those who have substantial amounts of money to put aside for a number of years and have exhausted their allocation of savings certificates.

This is not for the smaller saver both because the amounts required are fairly substantial and the withdrawal provisions are strict. Also because better rates are currently available from savings certificates and SAYE. The rates for short-term lending are not competitive at the moment. Local authority loans will not, of course, fit in with a regular savings plan.

Local authority loans

● have good interest rates for the larger saver, but it does lock up your money for quite a time.

Premium bonds have always been a controversial part of the

How it works

Local Authority Loans

Interest
Varies. Current rates are between 7% and $8\frac{1}{2}\%$
Minimum Investment
Varies. Rarely less than £100. Often £1,000
Withdrawal Terms
Vary between 1 and 10 years
Tax Points
Income tax is deducted before payment of interest

Is it for me? Should I save in a local authority loan?

For

Against

Premium bonds

National Savings movement because they offer the saver some of the joys of gambling. Instead of interest, premium bond holders have a regular chance to win a cash prize.

It is a special sort of gamble since you run no risk of losing the money staked. But you do stand to lose all the income you might have got from your money if you had saved it elsewhere. And you will remember the frightening graph on page 11, which showed how inflation is eroding the real value of your money. These days you need to earn interest on your savings just to keep their real value steady.

It has been estimated that if you hold your full allocation of bonds – £1,250 – you stand a good chance of winning at least one prize each year. This, however, is likely to be only £25 – larger prizes are far more rare – and this represents interest of only 2% on £1,250 (3·4% taxable).

How it works
- Bonds can be bought at the post office in units of £1. The bonds themselves are of a variety of denominations. They are denominated in different numbers of units, each unit representing one chance in the prize draw.

- Each month nearly 60,000 prizes are given, ranging in value from £25 to one bumper prize of £50,000. Each week there is a draw for one prize of £25,000.

- The selection of prize winners is done by the electronic sorting device, Ernie. Your bonds are entered in the draw after they have been held for three clear months.

- If you are one of the lucky ones, you will be notified of your win through the post, and the prize-winning numbers also appear in the newspapers.

WISEGUIDE

Only if you like a gamble.

Chapter 3

Borrowing and getting credit

Many people still believe quite simply that saving is good and borrowing is bad. They regard getting into debt as little short of a scandal, with the big exception of using a building society for a home mortgage. It is unlikely that Polonius' advice to his son in Shakespeare's play *Hamlet* – "neither a borrower nor a lender be" – did the young man much good in the long run. But it is a point of view which is still widely held.

All the same, more and more people deliberately run into debt every year. In Britain we owe between us over £1,400m. of instalment credit to hire purchase companies, department stores and the like. We owe over £9,000m. to building societies, while personal overdrafts at the banks have at some times topped the £1,000m. mark.

Don't be afraid to borrow if you need to.

WISEGUIDE

● Borrowing or getting credit is, like anything else, beneficial when used in moderation, dangerous when taken to excess.

Points to watch

The oldest joke about credit is that money is only lent to people who don't need it in the first place. There is more than a grain of truth in this. Anyone who lends money naturally wants to be pretty sure that he will get it back in time. So he will be inclined only to lend "on security". In such a case the borrower must have some possessions which the lender could claim and sell in the event of a default.

Security is still valued highly by lenders, but they no longer limit their field of acceptable borrowers to "men of property". Since 1945 two dramatic changes in attitude and practice have taken place.

● 1) Lenders have come to realise that earning power can be just as good a form of security as existing wealth. In other words, the man who has a reasonable income and good prospects, but who needs more money than he has at hand in order to buy a car, can be just as good a credit risk as the man who already owns a house and a few thousand shares. He may even be a better credit risk. As a sober and responsible family man he may be less likely to overreach himself and go bankrupt, or flee

the country, than the wealthy speculator.

● 2) Lenders have appreciated that they can provide themselves with security for their loan by keeping an interest in the goods bought with their money. As we shall see, this is an area fraught with legal difficulties. That is why hire purchase has grown up at such a fast rate since the war, because under a hire purchase contract the lender and not the purchaser actually remains the owner of the goods until the debt is fully paid.

As a result of developments such as these, buying on credit has become a part of everyday life. Yet the old attitudes survive. "Live now, pay later" is hardly a complimentary way to describe the hire purchase era, and many commentators on the social scene still believe that if a thing is worth owning it is worth saving up for.

Yet nowadays such advice is just not practicable. If you started to save for the price of your house from scratch you would probably be ready to move into an old people's home by the time you had the right amount. But if it is reasonable that you should borrow to buy a house, is it equally reasonable to borrow to buy a car, or a refrigerator, or a holiday or even a new suit?

WISEGUIDE

Borrowing means being prepared to give up some of your future income in order to have the use of something you want now rather than later. You must realise that if you borrow now, you must pay for the privilege. By the time your car or suit is paid for, it will have cost you rather more than if you had paid immediately in cash. In other words, just as you earn interest when you save, you must pay interest when you borrow.

There is another catch. It is easier to spend money that you don't have than to spend money which you have to count out from your own purse. Credit facilities are so widely available that the temptation to overreach yourself can be great.

This argument cuts two ways. If you can't buy a major durable item like a refrigerator on credit you may very well never get around to buying it at all. Unfortunately this does not mean that the money will be spent instead on something equally useful. It may well just be frittered away. So although credit can make budgeting more difficult, it can just as well make it easier instead. Once you have bought the refrigerator on credit you are bound to put aside the repayment sum every week, so some of your budgeting is done for you. As long as the original decision to buy on credit was a sound one it can help to make life both easier and fuller for those who do it.

WISEGUIDE   Using credit properly can make your life easier.

Finance houses, like banks, whose lending activities are discussed in Chapter 4, are not actually defined in law. However, there are about 1,000 institutions actively engaged in providing instalment credit finance. They do not only provide hire purchase finance, nor was that their original function, but it does represent the major part of their business. A handful of large companies now dominate the trade and many of them have diversified into commercial and overseas finance. But the only important diversification which is relevant to the individual's use of money is the provision of personal loans.

Borrowing facilities available

In hire purchase transactions the upper limit on the amount advanced is set on two considerations:

Points to remember

- The price of the goods being bought.

- The financial standing of the borrower.

These are in addition to the finance houses' overall ability to lend, which again depends on how much money it raises from the public, and on any official Government lending controls in force at the time. These may set a limit on the total amount by which a finance house can increase its lending, but in themselves they will not fix a limit on the size of individual advances.

The point about hire purchase is that, strictly speaking, it does not involve a loan at all. The finance house buys the goods from the retailer and the "buyer" hires them from the finance house, only "buying" them when he pays his last instalment. This has some legal implications, but for practical purposes hire purchase is simply the most widely used form of consumer credit.

What H.P. really means

Under current law (discussed more fully in chapter 17) the Government can require that part of the cost of goods bought by hire purchase has to be provided at the outset by the buyer. For example, if you want to buy a £1,000 car on hire purchase, you might have to pay an initial deposit of 40% of the price.

The extent of this minimum deposit is liable to be changed from time to time because successive governments have believed that such changes provide the most quick and effective way of controlling the amount we spend. The size of the deposit varies depending on what you are buying.

Until recently, cars were subject to the 40% requirement. The general figure for goods subject to control orders was $33\frac{1}{3}$%, but for furniture, 20%, and for cookers and water heaters, 10%

The restrictions, however, were lifted in July 1971.

The minimum deposit is only one prong of the fork of official control orders. The other is the maximum repayment period.

Until July 1971, money advanced by the hire purchase company had to be paid back within 24 months for all goods subject to the orders except cookers and water heaters (48 months).

The control orders cover virtually everything that the average household is likely to buy on hire purchase. If it chooses to buy

a hearse or a mobile canteen it will be free from the orders. But if it is more conventional and uses hire purchase to buy cars, washing machines, three-piece suites and similar items it will have to observe them. The Crowther Committee has recommended that these control orders are abolished.

WISEGUIDE

● One limit on the amount that you can borrow is set by the control orders, which apply to hire purchase contracts and to any other form of credit sale.

● The finance house is also bound to take your individual credit-worthiness into account in deciding how much – if anything – it is prepared to lend to you.

How it works

It is important to bear in mind that the finance house does not normally have a personal relationship with the borrower. It does not have the sort of detailed information and opinion about a customer's credit standing that a bank manager would have. As a general rule the finance house will only be introduced to the customer through the seller. It will build up a trading relationship with the shop or garage, who will channel all their applications for credit facilities through to it. In deciding whether to grant the loan the finance house will rely on the form that the prospective borrower has filled in, the references that he has provided and any information available about his general credit-worthiness.

A "clean" record

Information of this kind is provided by credit reference bureaux such as British Debt Services Ltd. and the United Association for the Protection of Trade Ltd. Their job is to keep records of all debt recovery actions in the courts and any other information that might suggest that a loan was unlikely to be repaid. A finance house which has an unsatisfactory experience with a customer may very well pass that fact on to one of the bureaux.

If what appears to be a reasonable loan application is turned down, it may very well be because one of these bureaux has reported something unfavourable about the customer. Mistakes can happen – especially if the previous occupier of your address happened to be a bad credit risk. One of the Crowther Committee's proposals is that these bureaux should be obliged to pass on any "black" information about a member of the public to him, so that he has a chance to prove that it is false.

Even if you have a "clean" record the finance house will clearly set some limit on the amount that it is prepared to lend to you. The main standard will, of course, be your apparent ability to make the regular weekly or monthly repayment.

In 1969 only 20% of those who used hire purchase and similar forms of credit were making weekly repayments of more than £2. Obviously, in some cases, even that amount could prove a burden and there is a small proportion of borrowers who accumulate debts which are well beyond their ability to repay. The

lender will do his best to take means and existing indebtedness into account when deciding whether to advance the amount required and he will obviously do more checking if the nature of the customer's job or some other factor suggests that he might prove a bad credit risk. Whether a customer is overreaching himself must be his decision rather than the finance house's.

WISEGUIDE

Do not take on more hire purchase commitments than you can reasonably afford, bearing in mind all the other calls on your money.

Credit sales

Most of the points made so far also apply when credit sale rather than hire purchase is used, but in a credit sale the legal ownership of the goods passes straight to the buyer, who repays the loan in five or more instalments (see also chapter 17 on the legal situation). The finance house loses out in terms of security but may well gain in terms of simplicity. For many smaller transactions, where security is not regarded as very important, credit sales are increasing in popularity. They are, however, subject to some Government control orders.

Hire purchase law is remarkably complicated. Remember that the law may change soon.

Points to watch

● Anyone who signs a hire purchase agreement has a right to cancel the transaction and recover his first payments within a limited period unless he has signed at the premises of the dealer or finance house.

● A customer can terminate the agreement by writing at any time. But he may be liable to pay not only all accrued arrears but also an amount which takes his total payments up to half the purchase price.

● A finance house cannot terminate a hire-purchase agreement unless it has served a notice of default giving the customer seven days to pay the arrears. If a third of the hire purchase price has been paid the finance house will need court approval to repossess the goods.

● Any member of the public who, in good faith, buys a car that in fact already belongs to a finance house under a hire purchase agreement cannot have the car taken away from him.

Of the many provisions of the hire purchase acts, only six apply to credit sales. The most important is the right to cancel an agreement. A hire purchase agreement makes the finance house largely responsible for the "fitness and quality" of the goods, but the buyer's protection is far smaller under a credit sale agreement. He simply has the limited rights conferred on him by other acts – and even these can be excluded by the contract. The fact that you can turn for redress to a finance house if goods bought

under a hire purchase agreement are unsatisfactory is an important advantage of that type of contract.

WISEGUIDE

Know the law, and know your rights and responsibilities under it.

Until 1969 credit sales were undoubtedly cheaper for the customer than hire purchase deals, because the interest the buyer paid was eligible for tax relief. The 1969 Budget ended that and it remains to be seen whether the present Government will eventually restore this tax relief, which has never been available for hire purchase payments. If they do, credit sales could become even more widely used.

Personal loans

A rapidly expanding area of finance house activity is the personal loan. Here the finance house gives up all interest in security and simply lends a customer a sum of money which may be used for any of a wide variety of purposes. In a way they are taking over and making respectable the old moneylender's business.

Normally they will want to know how the customer intends to spend the money: whether it will be used to buy a washing machine or pay for a holiday in France. Strictly speaking, they should see that personal loans are not used to get round hire purchase control orders, but that is easier said than done. The fact is that a personal loan is not only cheaper than hire purchase finance (largely because it is simpler to operate) – it is also often available in larger amounts simply because the control orders do not apply in practice. The major finance houses will commonly make personal loans of up to about 18 times the planned monthly repayment, and the total sum involved is usually not less than £100.

WISEGUIDE

A personal loan is worth trying for if you need (and can afford to repay) a minimum of £100.

The costs of credit

These are hard to measure and are a general problem which affects the whole field of credit. The Crowther Committee wants to see far stricter provisions regarding disclosure of true credit costs. At the moment only a contract with moneylenders has to state the true rate of interest. This would have to be stated by a finance house if it made reference to interest rates in their hire purchase advertising. Few of them do.

At the moment all that the buyer can do in most cases is to compare the cash price with the credit price. But the cost of the credit will depend on more than the difference between these two figures. It will also have to take account of the length of the

repayment period and the number of instalments.

An example: If goods with a cash price of £100 are available under credit terms for £110 the real cost of the credit would be $9\frac{3}{4}\%$ a year if 24 monthly repayments were made and $20\frac{1}{2}\%$ if 52 weekly repayments were made.

● At the moment it is almost impossible for the ordinary man to "shop around" and find the cheapest form of credit available. The average hire purchase contract currently involves a real rate of interest of about 20% when a car is being purchased.

● There are plenty of small finance houses which advertise personal loans in the press. They can often charge very much more than 20%, though by "compensation" they often get the worst customers.

WISEGUIDE

As a general rule, the more the instalments and the smaller the total repayment period, the higher the real cost of the credit will be.

Check traders

Check trading developed naturally from the mutual clubs in the industrial centres of the North of England. It is one of the simplest of all forms of credit. The check trader issues checks to his customers who use them to buy a wide variety of goods at a long list of shops. Suppose a check has a face value of £50. The buyer will pay the check trader, say, 5p in the pound – £2·50 in this case – each week for 21 weeks. The check can be used to purchase goods up to its face value.

When the seller presents the check to the check trader to get the money back several weeks later he will have a discount of up to 15% deducted. He is presumably willing to accept this because check trading allows him to do business that he would not otherwise get. And the discount allows the check trader to keep the charges on his customers low. The system is quite different from hire purchase, where the finance house often pays a commission to the motor dealer for introducing business to it. All the same, the real cost to a customer of check trading is not cheap. If he pays back 5% more than the face value of his check, as in the example above, his credit is actually costing him a *nominal* annual interest rate of about 25%.

The *real* annual rate is even higher, but for many people the price is worth paying; check trading makes credit available to people who might find it hard to raise a personal loan and do not want to make the large purchases typically associated with hire purchase contracts. Moreover, the system has other attractions. Check traders employ agents who visit customers both to sell checks and to collect repayments. They get to know their customers personally and will usually be prepared to postpone collections in case of hardship.

As people have become better off, some of the check traders have developed a scheme known as voucher trading. Vouchers are made out in larger amounts than checks and the repayment periods are longer. But they share with checks the advantage of not being subject to hire purchase control orders. So you can use a check or voucher to pay the whole price of a washing machine, where under hire purchase or credit sale agreements you would have to put up a third of the price yourself.

For those on lower incomes check trading can be a useful way of getting credit. But remember, it is not cheap.

Pawnbrokers

Hardly surprisingly, pawnbroking is a dying trade. Where less than £2 is lent the pawnbroker can automatically take full possession of the goods six months and a week after they were pawned. If the figure is over £2 he has to sell the goods by public auction. His maximum profit on a loan is set in law at ½p for each 25p lent. But when charges, valuation fees and so forth, are added in the real cost of a loan from a pawnbroker can be very high.

Of the goods pledged, jewellery is most commonly used, but radios, tape recorders and the like are catching up fast. The average amount lent tends to be between £1 and £4, and about half the loans made are used to overcome temporary but severe financial difficulties.

WISEGUIDE

Only pawn your valuables when all other attempts to get money fail.

Moneylenders

Unlike pawnbroking, money-lending is still going strong. There are about 2,500 licensed money-lenders and many more who have managed to avoid becoming licensed. The commonest money-lenders' loans appear to be about £100 to £150, but interest rates vary immensely. If the loan is secured on some possession of the borrower's the annual rate is likely to be 20–30%, but where it is unsecured the rate may rise to 50% or even more. The average figure is probably about 40%. About a third of all loans are taken to cover exceptional outlays, such as weddings or holidays, while a further third is used to pay bills during periods of financial difficulty.

The moneylender is very much at the end of the credit line. His loans are expensive, but he will at least consider any application. Moreover, he tends to deal with people who are, by nature of their financial position and status in society, unable to turn elsewhere for help.

WISEGUIDE

Money-lenders should only be used as a last resort.

Small loan societies

Mutual self-help in financial affairs has never really caught on in Britain. However, a number of loan societies of one sort or another have taken root. They tend to lend small sums to their members for short periods at fairly low rates of interest. Among them are small loan companies, which are on the decline, friendly societies, only a few of which lend on any scale, and non-profitmaking credit unions.

WISEGUIDE

Quite a good idea if you can find them.

Life assurance companies

If you have an endowment policy in force it may be possible to raise a loan from your assurance company. After a few years at the most such policies have what is known as a surrender value and the amount that can be borrowed is usually fixed as a percentage of this. The interest rate is usually low, because the loan is perfectly secure from the assurance company's point of view, and the money can be used for any purpose. Repayment is a matter for negotiation: indeed, it can be possible to keep the whole of the loan outstanding until the life policy matures. The loan will then be deducted from the sum payable.

WISEGUIDE

This can be a useful form of credit for anyone who needs to make an exceptional outlay but does not want actually to surrender, or terminate, his life policy.

Second mortgage lenders

The second mortgage business is one of the fastest growing areas of credit. The principle involved is simple enough: many owner occupiers have houses which have risen sharply in value as they have been paying off their main mortgage. As a result they can support further borrowing, and it is the second mortgage firms which provide it. They tend to act as brokers, making certain that the prospective borrower really does own the interest in his property that he says he does and that he has the ability to make repayments. The second mortgage firms then recommend the loan to a finance house, life assurance company or similar financial institution.

Points to remember

- This is a field where the borrower needs to know what he is doing.

- There are some second mortgage brokers who are adept at forcing more credit on the borrower than he really wants, or imposing excessive service charges.

- The rate of interest that is charged is usually very much higher than that on a first mortgage. Rates occasionally reach 25%, while a building society mortgage costs only $8\frac{1}{2}\%$.

WISEGUIDE

You should only raise a second mortgage if you cannot obtain the credit you want direct from a finance house, bank or similar institution. Even then you should "shop around" and pay close attention to all the small print. Otherwise you may find the cost prohibitive.

Mail order houses

Mail order firms, like finance houses, come in a wide variety of shapes and sizes. Some are among the largest companies in the land. Others are virtually one-man businesses. But as far as credit is concerned, only the major "catalogue houses" are relevant here. These are the firms which rely on sending out glossy catalogues of goods for sale in order to attract their customers. Most of them work through paid agents.

Credit prices only

More people are thought now to use mail order credit than any other kind – including hire purchase – though the sums involved are, of course, often far smaller. The fact that the mail order houses grew out of the old Victorian shop clubs means that they operate for the most part on a "credit-only" basis. They rarely quote cash prices, only credit prices, and if you want to pay by cash you are unlikely to be offered a discount for so doing.

This naturally makes it difficult to measure what the cost of the credit is in terms of interest per cent. The normal way in which the houses operate is to require payment for the goods sold in 20 equal weekly instalments: probably only 20% or so of their credit is extended for longer terms, with 38 weeks a not uncommon repayment period when more expensive items are involved.

A huge army of agents are on the big houses' lists. They consist mainly of housewives who drum up business from their friends and neighbours and earn themselves a 10% commission for doing so.

One mail order company alone has a million agents on its list, so obviously they cannot all be screened and vetted perfectly. But the majority are honest, conscientious and efficient. The commission they receive obviously has to be paid ultimately by the customer, yet it is difficult to tell how much more expensive it is to buy goods on credit from mail order houses than to buy them for cash from the shops.

But mail order can be cheap

Ironically, in some cases mail order goods are cheaper than cash ones in the shops. This is because these firms have lower overheads to meet than shops and this goes some way towards offsetting the cost of the agents' commissions and of supplying the credit to the buyer. However, those goods which are genuinely cheaper may be no more than "loss leaders", branded goods which can be compared directly with identical ones for sale in the shops. The price to be paid for the non-branded goods is probably anywhere between 5 and 15% higher than the price of a similar product in the shops. It is for the customer to decide whether this extra amount is worth paying: he or she should bear in mind such advantages as direct delivery of the goods to the house, a generally high standard of quality and money-back guarantees.

WISEGUIDE

Buying through mail order can be an effective way of using credit, but it is not for those who like to see and touch the goods they are buying before committing themselves.

Shops

If you walk out of a shop with goods that you have not paid for, you are either a shoplifter, or the receiver of credit. Leaving aside the first possibility, it is still clear that the average shopper uses credit of one sort or another almost every day of his or her life. A lot of this credit is completely random and unregulated: items are simply "put on the bill" and the bill is settled in a matter of days, weeks or a month or two at the most. No contract is signed and no interest is charged.

WISEGUIDE

Bills have to be paid eventually and in your own interest you should not let yourself take too much advantage of this sort of facility.

Ordinary accounts

Sometimes the relationship between the shopkeeper and the shopper is formalized when the shopper has to sign a form in order to open an account. Bills will tend to be presented for settlement on a more regular basis, but so far it is not normal for interest to be charged on such an account. However, this may come in time as more and more shops (especially the larger ones) realise that they are in effect subsidizing the credit-payer. At the very least they are likely to make more use of the cash discount – selling goods at a cheaper price if payment in cash is made at once.

Budget accounts

A more formal arrangement still is what is known as the "budget account", of which there are many varieties. Basically you agree to make a regular monthly payment of, say £5, and are allowed in return to buy goods worth up to eight times this amount, or £40. As each £5 payment is made, so new purchases are allowed as long as the outstanding balance is never more than £40. With budget accounts interest is usually charged to the buyer, though it is generally incorporated in what is known as a service charge. This may well amount to 5% of the amount outstanding at the end of each month.

Credit where Credit's due.

Personal Loans
Minimum loan £100.
Worth trying for.

Check Trading
For people who'd find it hard to
raise a personal loan.
For small purchasers only.

Pawnbrokers
Only if all else fails.

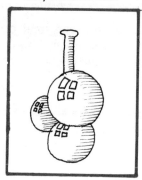

Money Lenders
Very high interest rates. Should
definitely be avoided.

Small Loan Societies
Quite good if you can find them.
Low rates.   Short term.

Life Assurance Societies
Repayment Negotiable.
Low interest rates.

Second Mortgage
High interest rate.
Know what you're doing.

Mail Order
Can be cheap.

Shops
Remember that you have to pay
it all back in the end.

Quite an expensive way of using credit, but it is convenient, and one which allows you to budget easily.

Option accounts

A more recent alternative to the budget account is the option account. Here the customer has the option of paying his account in full when he or she receives the bill, in which case no interest is charged. Alternatively, he or she can decide to pay by instalments, and these will include credit charge. The amount of this charge can vary widely from shop to shop, but the minimum instalment is usually a fifth of the outstanding balance.

Naturally, many of the major types of credit already mentioned in this chapter are made available at shops. Thus it is often possible to buy goods on hire purchase or credit sale from a shop, though it will often in fact be a finance house rather than the shop which is supplying the credit. And, of course, it is not only shops which supply the credit described in recent paragraphs. One can run up an account with a builder, a hotel, a milkman and a travel agent – not to mention the electricity and gas boards, and the Post Office, who bill on a quarterly basis for services used all the time.

Some rules for using credit

It will be clear by now that you have to keep a clear head nowadays if you are to make the best use of all the credit facilities which are available. The two questions to ask yourself are:

● How much credit should you use at any time?

● What sort of credit should it be?

There are no hard and fast answers to either question. In answering the first you have to think primarily about the future repayments to which you are committing yourself. *For the average household, an average monthly outlay in credit repayments of more than about a quarter of its wages or salaries would probably be unwise*, though there will clearly be exceptions to this rule.

In choosing how you will borrow, you will have to take into account both cost and convenience. At the moment the *real* cost of credit is often very difficult to measure precisely. As we have seen, it depends not only on the difference between the cash price and the credit price, but also on the length of the repayment period and the number of instalments to be repaid.

How to work out real credit costs simply and fairly accurately

Suppose you borrow £20 and have to repay eight quarterly sums of £3 – or £24 in all. The difference between the two amounts is £4 – 20% of £20. The repayment period is two years, so divide the figure of 20% by two to get a crude annual rate of interest – 10%. Then multiply by 1·8 to take account of the fact that the outstanding loan is being reduced each quarter. If the repayments are monthly, rather than quarterly, you should multiply

by 1·9, and by 2 if repayments are weekly. These sums may seem daunting, but they are worth doing if large sums are involved. In the example given earlier in this paragraph the true annual rate of interest would be not 10 but somewhere between 18 and 20% (10 × 1·8; or 10 × 1·9; or 10 × 2·0).

WISEGUIDE

If the cost of borrowing seems to be excessive take the trouble to shop around and see if you cannot get what you need for less. Sometimes, however, it will be worth while.

Some exceptions

Paying a little over the odds for convenience. Suppose you are buying a car. Perhaps you could raise a personal loan at under 20% for the amount involved. But it may well be very much simpler to use the slightly more expensive hire purchase facilities that are available at the motor dealer's own offices. A formal credit sale may be cheaper than the revolving credit extended by your shopkeeper, but the latter may well be more convenient to you. You should remember that the so-called interest charge also includes the cost of providing other aspects of the credit service – the mail order or check traders' agents' commissions, for example. These are services you may be prepared to pay for in their own right because they make shopping easier for you.

WISEGUIDE

The basic rules, then, are very simple. Don't over-extend yourself. Count the real cost. And choose the type of credit that suits you best.

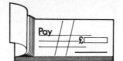

Chapter 4

Banking

Making the most of your account

"But I don't have a bank account," says the perplexed gentleman in one bank's cinema advertisement. "Then you should have," is the inevitable reply.

Should you, and if so, what sort of account should it be?

The second question is just as important as the first, because there is quite a wide range of banking facilities to choose from nowadays. It is as well to get some basic points clear before examining these facilities in detail.

Broadly speaking, banks perform two distinct functions:

What banks do

- Supplying a money transmission service

- Borrowing and lending.

So a bank account opens three major possibilities to the ordinary account holder.

1) He can move money from one place to another without having to handle any cash.
2) He can leave money with the bank for safe-keeping and earn interest on it.
3) He can borrow money from the bank.

Banks do, of course, provide other services as well: they act as executors and trustees, for example, and can help you to manage your investments. But these are secondary to the main services.

A bank account can simplify your financial transactions.

WISEGUIDE

There are, of course, plenty of other institutions which are not banks but which provide at least some of these major services. Building societies, for example, will look after your money for you and pay you interest while they do so. All the finance houses are in business to lend you money, either directly or in the form of hire purchase sales, and some of them will offer you interest on your savings as well. But neither building societies nor finance houses operate a money transmission service. Therefore they can hardly be said to be in the business of banking.

Points to watch

In the field of borrowing and lending the degree of overlap between banks and other institutions such as these is considerable. Therefore it is important to relate what is said in this chapter to chapters 2 and 3 which cover savings and credit. If you are simply looking for a home for your money, or want to

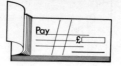

borrow some, then it is in those chapters that you will probably find the right answer to your problems. But if you are interested in the other facilities that a bank has to offer – notably the cheque book facility – then you may well find it convenient to save with the bank or borrow from it as well.

Most of this chapter will be concerned with the so-called "clearing banks" – the big high street banks whose names are household words even to non-customers. But they are not alone in providing money transmission services. Separate sections later on will deal with the National Giro and the Trustee Savings Banks which compete with the clearing banks in at least some of their transmission activities. It is obviously impossible to say which of them is the "best buy" because so much will depend upon the individual customer's needs. But a description of what they all have to offer, and what it costs, will allow you to form your own judgement.

WISEGUIDE

A bank account may *not* be the best thing for your needs. Read the next section carefully.

The clearing banks

In England and Wales five banks handle the business of the overwhelming majority of private bank account holders. In order of size they are: National Westminster (3,600 branches) Barclays (3,200), Midland (2,700), Lloyds (2,300) and Williams and Glyns (300). Together with the banking firm of Coutts and Co. (a subsidiary of the National Westminster) they are the only real clearing banks and this section will naturally concentrate on what they have to offer.

However, there are a few other banks which cover broadly the same ground as the clearing banks do and which will therefore also be referred to from time to time in this section. The most important of them are the Co-operative Bank and the Yorkshire Bank. Shoppers in the West End of London will also be familiar with Lewis's Bank in Selfridges and the banking department of Harrods. Both offer banking facilities of the sort described here. Indeed, there is a host of small, private banks of one sort or another, but very few of them have a significant number of personal account holders.

To anyone who lives or travels in Scotland the familiar names will be the Bank of Scotland, the Clydesdale and the Royal Bank of Scotland: the former now includes the British Linen Bank and the latter the National Commercial Bank of Scotland. Once again, much of what is said in this section will apply to them, though there are some significant differences in banking practice.

Transmitting money

As we said earlier, one of the main tasks of a bank is to provide a *money transmission service*. This phrase needs some explaining. All cash is money (provided it is still legal tender)

but not all money is cash. Daily life would be impossible if it were. Imagine the problems of an important industrialist having to pay for a £5,000,000 factory in dirty one pound notes. Even if he was physically capable of picking them up, he could hardly send them by post to the contractor a hundred miles away. Naturally, he uses banking facilities to move his money about.

Is he so very different from the private individual? There must be many people without bank accounts who have had to carry large sums of money around from time to time and the few hundred yards between your house and your motor dealer may seem like miles of bandit-infested mountains if you have a £400 down payment for your car in your wallet. An even more common problem is that of sending money to a relative or friend: you either have to take the risk of putting cash in the post or make the trek to the nearest post office to buy a postal order.

Carrying cash around unnecessarily is a foolish thing to do. **WISEGUIDE**

Writing a cheque

POINTS TO NOTE

Check the date
Check the name of the payee
Check the amount in the space provided with the pence in the figures.

five pounds 23. £5-23
five pounds 03. £5-03
five pounds only £5-
  or £5-00
Twenty three pence £0-23
  or 23p

Write in figures in the box. Banks today advise you to use a hyphen and not a decimal point; if necessary, place one figure between the pound sign and the hyphen; **always** place two figures after the hyphen.

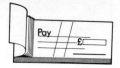

A current account   With a current account at a bank matters can be much easier. The way in which it operates is really perfectly simple. You can open a current account with any sum from a few pounds upwards. In return you will be provided with a cheque book. This is more than a symbol of affluence. In a steadily increasing number of everyday transactions cheques can be used as freely as cash. This is how a typical transaction works:

Assume you owe the gas board £20.

1) Instead of walking down to the board's offices and handing over the amount in cash, you write out a cheque. It is in fact no more than a written instruction to your bank to pay £20 on your behalf, docking that amount from the balance of your current account.

2) Because you have written the name of the gas board on the cheque it is only the gas board who can receive payment. Therefore it is perfectly safe to put the cheque in an envelope and post it. Even if it is stolen, it will be no good to anybody since it will hardly be easy for the thief to masquerade as a gas board. *So the cheque will never be presented for payment and you will lose nothing.*

3) On receiving the cheque the gas board will take it to their own bank which will credit the £20 to the board's account.

4) The cheque will then be sent to London where it will be "cleared".

It would obviously be ridiculous for, say, Lloyds to have to pay separately for every cheque drawn by one of its customers and receive separate payment for every cheque drawn by customers of another bank in favour of one of its customers. So the system is centralized: all the cheques are totted up and each bank makes or receives just one payment to or from its competitors.

5) When the cheque has been cleared, it will be returned to the branch of the bank on which it was drawn – your branch, in other words. There your account will be reduced by £20 – assuming that the balance is worth at least £20 in the first place. If not, the bank will either allow you to become overdrawn and go into the red, or refuse to honour your cheque. It is perfectly at liberty to do the latter unless you have already arranged an overdraft limit. If it does so, the cheque will be returned to the payee and it will be his job to take up the matter with you and force you to pay in an acceptable way.

To keep good relations both with your bank and with those to whom you have to pay cheques, it is essential to make sure that you never go into the red unwittingly.

A valuable facility

The ability to pay by cheque is probably the most important and valuable facility that a bank account affords you. But from the payee's point of view it is clearly essential to know that the cheque is in fact as good as cash to all intents and purposes. There are still many shopkeepers and the like who refuse to accept cheques, and many others who do so only grudgingly. But their number is decreasing.

The cheque cards

One reason for this is the introduction of the *cheque card*. All the clearing banks except Barclays are now prepared to make these available to their creditworthy customers. They are little plastic cards which can be shown to a shopkeeper or anyone else in order to allay his fears that the cheque may prove worthless.

They provide a guarantee that the payer's bank will honour any cheque up to the value of £30 regardless of the state of the payer's account. Strictly speaking, this facility ought to make cheques universally acceptable. In fact suspicion still remains. Some shops, restaurants and the like still expect payers to give their address as well as show their cheque card - this is really unnecessary. Others will not accept cheques at all.

If your bank refuses you a cheque card, you will have to rely on the honesty of your face and official-looking means of identification to get your cheques accepted. A driving licence remains the most popular identification of this sort. But a cheque card is better. Not only does it make your cheques more readily acceptable: it also allows you to draw cash from a bank when you are far from your own branch. For the cheque cards are in a standard form and all the banks who operate them are prepared to accept them from customers of other banks who want to draw cash at their branches.

A cheque card provides a guarantee of your creditworthiness. Try to get one.

WISEGUIDE

Standing orders

Cheques are not the only means by which a bank account allows you to make payments without using cash. For regular bills of a fixed amount a "standing order" can be the most sensible way of paying. You simply tell your bank, on a standard form which it will supply, that you want a certain sum paid from your current account to somebody else's account, say, every month or year. Where the amount is liable to vary, as with some insurance premiums,you can arrange for "direct debiting". This gives the insurance company the right to ask your bank branch to debit the appropriate amount from your account and credit it to his account whenever the premium falls due.

Any cheques, cash or money orders that you receive can be paid into your account without difficulty. If you are near to your own branch you can simply fill in a credit form and hand the

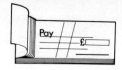

money over the counter. Or you can go into any other bank branch and fill in what is known as a "bank giro form". This has nothing to do with the National Giro run by the Post Office. It is simply a means of transferring money, whatever form it may take, from one bank branch to another. This means that not only can you have funds put into your own account but you can also go into a bank and arrange for money to be credited to somebody else's account – as long as you know his branch and account number.

Above all, any regular payments that other people make to you can go straight into your bank account. For most people this means their wages or salaries. Instead of having to queue up each week to receive your pay packet, the money can be credited directly to your account by standing order.

The main advantage of the services outlined so far is convenience, and in particular the fact that an account can help you to manage your financial affairs wisely. Cheque books contain counterfoils on which all outgoings can be recorded and banks send statements of accounts to their customers on a regular basis.

WISEGUIDE

Banks rarely make mistakes, but keep your own account of your transactions just in case the bank has made a mistake.

Services you must pay for

● You earn no interest on the money left in your current account. The fact that the money would earn interest elsewhere means that this is just as real a cost as —

● Bank charges. As for these, it is regrettably impossible to say exactly how great they are since only the Scottish banks publish a detailed and comprehensive tariff.

● However, about 20% of private bank customers are involved in group pay schemes which involve the direct payment of their wages or salaries into their accounts. For them the normal charges are fixed and they do not vary among the clearing banks.

Group terms

Under these "group terms" the customer pays no charge on up to 30 transactions a half-year as long as he holds £100 in his account. If this minimum balance is £50 he is charged 75p for a total of up to 30 transactions a half-year, the figure rising to £1·50 if the balance is less than £50. If he is one of those who needs more than 30 transactions a half-year he will be charged on an individual basis. These terms are subsidized by the employers who make a separate payment to the bank.

Ask your bank manager

If you are not covered by these terms you can always ask your bank manager to tell you the basis on which he charges you. You will find that the amount takes into account both the number of transactions – notably drawings of cash and payments by cheque – and the size of your balance. A common practice is to fix a

price for each transaction, under which standing orders and direct debits may well prove cheaper than cheque transactions, and then to allow a notional rate of interest on your current account balance.

Suppose you kept £100 in your account and this rate were 2%. That would mean that your bank manager would allow you £2 worth of free transactions before he started to charge you. Once you "ate up" this offsetting allowance you would probably find yourself paying about 6p–8p an item.

WISEGUIDE

It makes sense to find out about the basis of charging at an early stage, especially if you are shopping around to find the best bank for yourself. You may be lucky enough to avoid charges altogether. If you think your charges are too high, talk to your bank manager. He may cut them.

The credit card

There is one new and important side to the banks' transmission services that should be mentioned here and that is the *credit card*. This should not be confused with the cheque card, for it bypasses the need for cheques completely.

So far only Barclays operate one – the well-known Barclaycard. When buying goods or services anywhere a card is accepted, you present it, sign a slip and take your purchases away. Each month the bank presents you with a bill for settlement; normally you will pay by cheque. You do not have to be a Barclays customer to apply for a Barclaycard.

At the moment comparatively few outlets actually accept credit cards. But credit cards are almost certain to command wider acceptance in the future. And, as we shall see later in this chapter, they are a mechanism whereby bank customers can receive credit from their banks.

The banks' other services

So much for the transmission services. We can now look at the other main services that the bank performs – borrowing money from some customers and lending it to others. In addition to – or instead of – running a current account, which pays no interest, you can also open a deposit account, on which interest is paid up to the moment of withdrawal. At the moment all the clearing banks pay the same annual rate – 4%, or two percentage points below Bank rate. But it is quite possible that they will vary these rates in time. Deposit accounts are discussed in more detail in Chapter 2.

How banks use your money

The banks use the money left with them, in both current and deposit accounts, in three ways:

- Some is held in cash to meet customers' demands
- Some is invested, notably in Government bonds
- The rest is available for lending.

Most of the loans, however, are made to companies rather than individuals. And even if the banks wanted to step up their

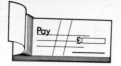

lending to the private customer, the Government and the Bank of England would very probably not allow a sharp increase. So the private customers who supply most of the banks' deposits get only about a tenth of their advances.

Getting an overdraft

It may not be easy to get an overdraft, as loans are called, but it is by no means impossible as long as you know the rules.

First: Realize that overdrafts are not meant to be long term loans. They are facilities designed to help the customer over a tricky period. For the individual, buying a house is the most obvious case in point. Suppose you have to complete on the purchase of your new house before receiving payment for the sale of your old one. That is when above all you need bridging finance and the chances are high that the bank would extend an overdraft in such a case. Or, on a smaller scale, you may have rather a lot of bills to pay one month. Your bank would be highly likely to allow you to move into the red in the knowledge that you would be in balance again once your next wage or salary cheque had come through.

Second: It is less likely that a bank will allow you to live beyond your means by granting you an overdraft facility. If you ask your bank manager for permission to run up a £500 overdraft he will want to know why you need the money, and he is unlikely to look sympathetically on such reasons as a desire to holiday in the south of France or to buy a colour television set. That, he may well say, is not what overdrafts are for.

Third: If he accedes to your request he is likely to ask for an assurance that the amount will be repaid quickly and for some security while the overdraft is outstanding. Something like share or unit trust certificates would normally be acceptable.

Fourth: Banks are, however, starting to make more money available to individuals and making it available for more wide-ranging purposes.

WISEGUIDE

Overdrafts are useful, but are generally only allowed for short periods.

Personal loans

In addition to their traditional overdraft facilities, all the major banks now have personal loan facilities as well. These differ from overdrafts in three important ways.

● *They are more expensive.* The rate of interest on your outstanding overdraft is unlikely to be more than three or four percentage points above Bank rate and may be less. So with Bank rate at 6% you are not going to pay more than 10% and may pay as little as $7\frac{1}{2}$% or 8%. The rate of interest on a personal loan from a bank may be expressed as a lower figure

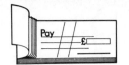

but it is charged on the original amount borrowed. It takes no account of subsequent repayments of the principal. So the *real* rates are usually higher than for overdrafts. Lloyds' scheme is the cheapest, at a real rate of 10%. All the others cost over 13%, but security is not necessary for any of them.

● *Repayment on a regular basis.* You contract to pay a fixed sum each month from the moment you take up your loan until it is clear. With an overdraft, repayment is a matter for negotiation with your bank manager. However, it is usually possible to phase repayment of a personal loan over one, two or even three years.

● *What you do with your loan is your business.* You can use it to pay for your holiday or T.V. set, though the bank may try to check that you are not using the loan to get round the hire purchase control orders. Moreover, you can borrow up to £1,000 – more than is usually possible on an overdraft.

Of the major banks, Barclays were the last to enter the personal loan field. But for some time before it had been possible for holders of Barclaycards to use them as credit facilities as well as cash substitutes. This is because Barclays allows the card holders to leave a sum, up to an agreed limit, unpaid at the end of the month: in most cases the limit is £100. However, if the amount due is left unpaid interest is charged at a real rate of over 18%.

Personal loans are a growing area of bank business. But remember that the interest rate charged can be high.

WISEGUIDE

Now that we have looked at the main services that the major banks provide a few general points should now be made.

Points to watch

First: Opening hours. Clearing banks are now open between 9.30 and 3.30 from Monday to Friday and some branches are open one evening a week as well. This means that you cannot draw cash or do anything else that involves visiting a branch at weekends, a serious disadvantage compared with National Giro and the Trustee Savings Banks for which the handful of automatic bank cash dispensers only partly compensates.

At the moment there are about 700 of these, mostly in the big towns. Barclays and National Westminster have each installed well over 200, Midland over 100 and Lloyds considerably fewer. They allow a customer to withdraw £10 by inserting a special card into a machine in the outside wall of the bank and "typing out" a code number. If a customer does not have access to such a machine and runs out of cash over the weekend he must hope either that his cheques will be accepted or, preferably, that someone will actually cash one for him.

Get a cash card if you can. They are useful in tiding you over emergencies.

Second: Service. The majority of customers – 87% according to a recent survey – are generally satisfied with this. But even among these people specific ideas about improvements are common. Apart from Saturday opening, many of them would like to see more frequent and detailed statements of account and more cashiers employed in busy periods. But if the banks accede to such requests bank charges will almost certainly rise as a result.

Third: The main reason for not opening an account in the first place is the belief that a bank is "not for people like me". Typical fears are that the staff will be unsympathetic, that shops will not accept cheques from a working man or woman, that a large initial balance is necessary, and that one would lose control of one's finances. None of these fears is justified, but that is not to say that everyone should have a bank account. You have to compare what the clearing banks have to offer and the price they charge, with the facilities available at the Giro or savings banks. This we shall now do.

WISEGUIDE

Current bank accounts would be useful for many people who do not have them at present. Check the following:

● Would you find a cheque book useful?
● Can your wage or salary be paid directly to the bank?
● Ask what your bank charges are likely to be. See if you can avoid them altogether.

The National Giro

The National Giro was set up by the Post Office as a means of providing a simple and cheap money transmission service. It was primarily designed for those who had no bank account, though, as it has turned out, existing bank customers account for most of the Giro's clientele.

What it offers

The Giro offers three basic facilities:

● It allows transfers of funds to other Giro account holders. You fill in a transfer form, which has your own name and address on it, with the details of what you want paid to whom and post it to the Giro's centre at Bootle. It costs you nothing. Standing orders for regular payments to account holders are also free.

● You can make deposits of cash or cheques into your own account at any post office without charge. Anyone else can pay money into your account at 3p a go.

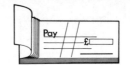

The National Giro

● You can withdraw cash from one of two designated post offices, again at 3p a time. The same charge is levied when you make payments to a non-account holder on a Giro cheque. A statement of account is posted to you after every transaction.

A Giro account is undoubtedly *cheaper* than a conventional bank account – especially since postage is free in the case of the former. The question is, *is it more convenient?* Giro came in for heavy criticism in its early days because the application forms were too complicated and the stationery (for which there is a small charge) too confusing. Improvements are being made in both respects, but another problem still remains.

This is the problem of acceptability. There is no point in having a Giro account, if people refuse to accept Giro cheques or transfers. The number of shops that do accept them is growing all the time, but it is still relatively small – certainly smaller than the number that accept bank cheques. However, cheques can be paid to people without Giro accounts. All they have to do is cash them at a post office or pay them into their bank accounts.

The Giro pays no interest on the money you deposit with it and is not allowed to make overdrafts. However, Giro account holders can apply for a personal loan from Mercantile Credit. If their application is successful they will pay a real rate of interest of about 19%, rather more than the cost of a personal loan from a clearing bank.

One major improvement that the Giro may eventually make in its services is to increase the number of post offices from which an account holder can withdraw cash. This could be effected by introducing some sort of cheque card along the lines of those supplied by the clearing banks. At the moment up to £20 can be withdrawn every other day, but larger sums can be withdrawn by prior arrangement. And, of course, post offices are open on Saturdays.

Comparison with a bank account

The Giro is still new, but in time it could emerge as a real rival to the clearing banks for the accounts of customers whose needs are not too sophisticated, simply because it is so much cheaper.

WISEGUIDE

As their name suggests, the trustee savings banks are first and foremost savings institutions. What they have to offer in this respect is discussed in the chapter on savings. But since 1965 they too have provided current account facilities. However, to be eligible for consideration as an account holder, you have already to be saving with a TSB. You either need £25 in your ordinary savings account or must have had such an account open for six years before you will be granted a current account, on which you can draw cheques. But if you pass this simple test you may be granted your cheque book and (at the manager's

Trustees Savings Bank

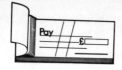

discretion) a cheque card as well.

Low charges No charge is levied if a cheque is used to draw cash, but a cheque made out to a third party carries a small "clearance charge" of 3p. This is paid to the major banks, for it is through their clearing system that TSB cheques have to pass.

No overdrafts All the major advantages of a bank account are available at TSBs with one striking exception: you cannot run up an overdraft. The TSBs themselves would, for the most part, like to be able to make loans but so far their request for Treasury permission to do so has not been granted. As an interim measure it is possible that some of them may come to an arrangement with a major finance house, under which the finance house rather than the TSB itself would extend the loan, along the lines of the Mercantile Credit/Giro scheme.

A TSB account is cheaper to run than a clearing bank account, but the absence of overdraft facilities may deter some prospective customers. Others may fear that a TSB cheque will be less widely accepted than one drawn on a well known bank, such as Barclays.

WISEGUIDE

1) Anyone who ● receives a weekly wage packet
● has his rent collected at the door
● pays for his gas and electricity by putting coins into a meter
● uses cash when shopping

probably has little use for a bank account or even a Giro account. But even for such a person there is little to lose by opening one, probably with the Giro rather than a bank because of the difference in charges. The services available may well come in useful one day.

2) For many other people the ability to pay by cheque or Giro transfer is of real benefit in making for a simple life. For those who would expect to pay little more than their service bills by cheque anyway the Giro is probably the better choice. But for those whose financial transactions are larger and more frequent a bank account is almost unavoidable.

3) For those who are really professional and sophisticated in managing their financial affairs, both types of account can be run in harness.

Chapter 5

Buying a House

Buying a house is probably the most important financial trans-action a married couple make in their lives. It is also one of the best and safest ways in the world to save and invest your money. Houses are the one form of investment that rarely lose in value, and at the rate house prices are rising today they come close to guaranteeing a capital growth that stays steadily ahead of infla-tion – in other words the value of your house is going up faster than the value of the pound in your pocket is going down. Prices of new houses have risen more than a third on average over the past five years, and prices of existing houses have gained up to 40% or more. Currently new houses are gaining in value at the rate of more than 6% a year on average, and existing houses are gaining at the rate of anything up to 8%. This means that the house you buy today may be worth quite a lot more than you paid for it in five years time, and even more – possible even twice as much – ten years from now.

You can see how house prices have risen from the table overleaf. One reason has been the steady rise in our standards of living. Bigger wage packets and the fact that more women stay at work after they are married means that young newlyweds can pay more for a house today than ever before. Half the new houses reaching the market every year are bought by couples making a home of their own for the first time. The government has also helped by making it easier for home buyers to raise bigger mortgages over longer repayment periods.

The other reason is that our small island only has a limited stock of houses to share out amongst all the people who are looking for homes of their own. Fifty years ago just one house in ten in Britain was owner-occupied, today the figure is one in every two. But the number of homes has barely doubled over the same period from $8\frac{1}{2}$m to $18\frac{1}{2}$m, and only about 500,000 houses – 200,000 of them new, and 300,000 existing houses – reach the market every year. That is less than 3% of the housing stock overall.

Buying a house should give you safe and steadily rising capital growth.

WISEGUIDE

You can benefit three ways from buying a house:

Home investment

● You can resell it again for more than you paid to make a *profit*.

Average new house prices 1961-70		
1961	£2,684	88
1962	£2,867	94
1963	£3,050	100
1964	£3,263	107
1965	£3,599	118
1966	£3,843	126
1967	£4,087	134
1968	£4,131	141
1969	£4,436	151
1970	£4,885	160

● You can cut out the cost of *rent*, because you or your descendents will eventually get back the money you pay on mortgage.

● You can divide it into flats or let off rooms to provide yourself with an *income*.

The table shows how steeply house prices have risen in the past five years, and why they are likely to climb even faster in the future.

But you may be able to do even better. The prices in the **table** were *average* prices, spread across a wide sample of homes from all over Britain.

Careful choice can enable you to do better than these trends. *You may even be able to make a bigger profit in a shorter period of time.*

Many things can help increase house values:

For

● Your district may become more fashionable and prices move up more than average.

● New communication links such as motorways can make an area more attractive to commuters.

● Improvements can turn a run-down property into a smart and attractive and much more valuable home.

● Prices in the London districts of Fulham and Barnsbury have rocketed as the smart set extends its frontiers. Houses in Islington that changed hands eight years ago for £3,500 now fetch up to £12,000 or more.

● The opening of the new M3 motorway has nearly doubled the prices of better homes in the Surrey commuter belt, with prices up from £7,000 to £11,000 or even £13,000 in less than five years.

● Extensive improvements to a small cottage at Slough have more than doubled its value from less than £2,500 to more than £5,000 in just over four years.

Against   You may lose money if you choose the wrong area – too near an airport, or new motorway – but these instances are very rare.

WISEGUIDE

Buying a house puts your money to work and should make you a handsome profit.

Rent   Paying rent can prove very expensive. If you have a flat that costs you £10 a week you will pay out £10,400 over twenty years. Your rent may well rise during the period, and at the end of the twenty years you will be left with nothing saved.

But if you buy a house you can pay the same amount towards a mortgage and find yourself at the end of twenty years owning your own home, completely free from debt.

Mr Average Home Buyer 1970

His Home

Average price – £4,956	
Average deposit – £1,229	
Average loans – £3,727	
Average monthly income – £137·20	
Average repayment – £30·85	

Four out of ten buyers in 1970 had already been owner-occupiers.

Three out of ten had been paying rent.

Another three out of ten had lived with relatives or friends.

Three out of ten moved because they were getting married; just over one in ten because they changed their jobs.

Nearly two out of ten wanted a bigger or better house.

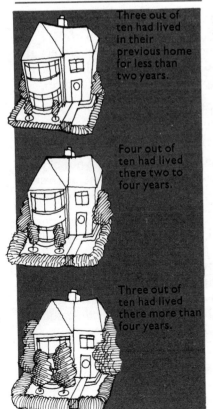

Three out of ten had lived in their previous home for less than two years.

Four out of ten had lived there two to four years.

Three out of ten had lived there more than four years.

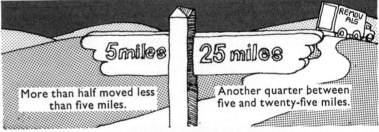

More than half moved less than five miles.

Another quarter between five and twenty-five miles.

Nearly another two out of ten bought detached houses.

Four out of ten bought semi-detached houses.

Two out of ten bought town houses or terraced homes.

Only six out of every hundred bought flats.

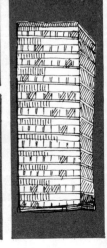

Make your money work for you and not for your landlord.

Income

You may be able to convert your house into flats or let off some of the rooms (and you may be able to get help from the local council towards the cost; see later in this chapter).

Self-contained flats in London easily earn more than £10 a week, residents at seaside resorts can let out rooms to summer visitors on a bed-and-breakfast basis at up to about £1·50 per night.

Consider the possible income you can earn from your home.

Safe and easy

● Buying a house is a comparatively *safe* way to invest. Unless you have enough money of your own to pay cash you will have to get a *mortgage*.

● The mortgage lender will almost certainly insist that you take out insurance to protect your home for the duration of the loan. If you are wise you will also make sure that you protect the mortgage and the furniture and other possessions that form the contents of your home (see chapter 00 on general insurance).

● It is also an *easy* way to invest. Once you get a mortgage you will be bound to repay the amount and the cost of the loan over a fixed number of years.

● The lender will make sure that the instalments are not beyond your means, and spreading your mortgage repayments over as many as thirty or even more years means that the monthly repayments will not wear too big a hole in your purse.

Tax concessions

You can even cut your tax bill because the government allows you to set off mortgage interest payments against tax.

You will also find that any profits you make from selling your house are *tax-free*. Owner-occupiers do not have to pay any tax on the profit they make from selling their homes unless they make a business of buying and selling houses. Each person (or husband and wife) is allowed only one tax-free "principal residence".

What can I buy?

Houses are divided into two main types as far as buying is concerned – new houses and existing houses. Each type then breaks down further into detached, semi-detached, and town houses or terraced homes, and if you like you can further sub-divide them according to the number of rooms (generally according to the number of bedrooms).

You can also build yourself a house, join a collective housing group, or buy a flat. If you are a tenant you may be able to buy your home on special terms.

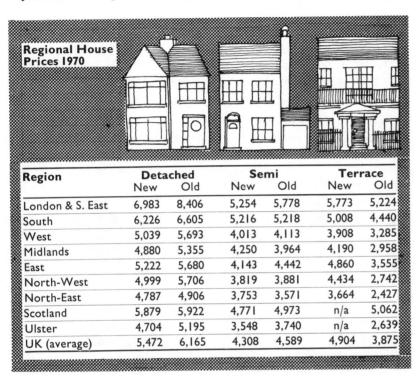

Regional House Prices 1970

Region	Detached		Semi		Terrace	
	New	Old	New	Old	New	Old
London & S. East	6,983	8,406	5,254	5,778	5,773	5,224
South	6,226	6,605	5,216	5,218	5,008	4,440
West	5,039	5,693	4,013	4,113	3,908	3,285
Midlands	4,880	5,355	4,250	3,964	4,190	2,958
East	5,222	5,680	4,143	4,442	4,860	3,555
North-West	4,999	5,706	3,819	3,881	4,434	2,742
North-East	4,787	4,906	3,753	3,571	3,664	2,427
Scotland	5,879	5,922	4,771	4,973	n/a	5,062
Ulster	4,704	5,195	3,548	3,740	n/a	2,639
UK (average)	5,472	6,165	4,308	4,589	4,904	3,875

Prices

Prices vary a great deal according to demand, which depends upon a great number of factors – including age, size, setting, and situation. But generally speaking prices are highest closest to the centres of big cities and fall away gradually as you travel out through the suburbs into the country.

You can see from the chart how the prices of various types of house differ across the country as a whole. London and the South-East was the most expensive area for three-bedroom detached houses in 1970, with prices ranging up to an average of £8,406 for an existing house or £6,983 for a new one.

Prices then drop away as one moves North and West, though Scotland was something of an exception. Northern Ireland was the cheapest area, with existing three-bedroom detached houses costing an average of £5,195 for an existing house and £4,704 for a new one.

> Existing houses are nearly always more costly than new houses, especially if they are detached or semi-detached. However new town houses are likely to cost more than existing ones, mainly because new town houses are mostly smart new developments in fairly expensive areas, whilst existing houses are generally older terraces.

Freeholds and Leaseholds

Most houses are sold freehold, that means that the owner has complete permanent control over both his house and the land on which it stands. But some may change hands on a leasehold basis, which means that the house and land go back to the land owner (the ground landlord) at the end of the lease.

Building Your Own

You can also build your own home. Most estate agents know of plots of land for sale, or you may see one advertised. But building your own house may prove a lot more expensive and more difficult to finance than buying one already built. If you do decide to build your own home make sure that you choose a builder who will give you a ten-year guarantee.

Housing Groups

You can also join a housing group to buy, build or modernise. The advantages of housing groups lie in the fact that they can spread the cost across several members instead of each member having to pay for everything himself. This means that they can also get far better mortgage terms – sometimes members only have to pay a £50 or a £100 deposit and repayments may be spread over as many as 60 years. But they also carry the disadvantage that members only get part of any increase in value when they leave, and they may have to accept certain communal restrictions – on pets, or hanging out their washing – and share certain communal maintenance costs.

Flats

Flats and maisonettes are really houses within houses. They can be cheaper than buying a whole house, especially in a big city. But they may also be harder to finance by a mortgage, and residents may have to accept the same sort of communal costs and restrictions as with housing groups.

Tenants

Tenants live in a housing world of their own as far as buying is concerned. If they are lucky and have long agreements at low rentals they may be able to purchase their freehold, or they may be entitled to buy it out under the terms of the Leasehold Reform Act. If they can, they will probably be able to secure their home for a figure quite a long way short of the normal market price.

What should I buy?

The right house for you will depend very much on your own personal likes and dislikes. You may prefer to pay more for a big house or a smart house or a house in the country even though you could buy something very much cheaper. The idea of buying a run-down old cottage might appeal to you as a great adventure and a chance to create a useful profit as well as an attractive home through modernisation. On the other hand it might strike you as a lot of hard work in unsavoury surroundings.

But most people have three basic rules. They want their house to be:
- The right price
- The right size
- In the right place

The Right Price

The right price is the amount you can afford to pay without straining your family budget. There is much more to buying a house than finding out the purchase price and the size of the mortgage deposit you will have to put down, and then taking one from the other.

There are also the cost of buying and the cost of running it.

You can read more about buying and running costs in a later section of this chapter, but remember that they can be fairly hefty.

For a start there are survey fees and legal bills when you buy the house. Then you may have to pay for repairs, or you may decide to redecorate. You may even decide to celebrate your move with new curtains, carpets, furniture and even a new washing machine. You may decide to instal central heating.

Once you have moved into your new home you have to pay the running costs. The biggest monthly bill will probably cover your mortgage repayment, but on top of that will come regular charges for gas, electricity, rates and water supplies, and possibly regular bills for a telephone or central heating.

If your new home is far from where you work or the nearest shops you may have to face sizeable bills for fares or car travel. You may have hire purchase repayments to meet, and every year you will almost certainly have to pay out something to keep your garden looking neat and trim.

WISEGUIDE

Remember the hidden costs when you look at house prices.

The Right Size

This largely depends on what you can afford and your family needs. Bigger houses cost more to buy and to run, but smaller houses can sometimes become very cramped over the years.

Two bedrooms may seem perfect for a young couple with no children when their in-laws come to stay, but could prove distinctly uncomfortable if they started a family. One living room might be enough for a family content to sit quietly around a television set in the evening, but far too little for a husband or wife seeking space for their hobbies.

WISEGUIDE

Allow for growth and budget accordingly.

The Right Place

The right place depends on the right house at the right price. The best way to solve this problem is to make a short list of the areas you prefer. Then comb through them, visiting local estate agents, reading local newspapers, driving round local streets that strike your fancy.

As soon as you have a list of houses you like start comparing them in terms of price, size and convenience (remote houses are cheaper, but they push up travel bills).

Then take a really close look at them. You ought to be able to spot any major defects fairly easily, and once you have selected the house that pleases you best you are ready to make an offer.

WISEGUIDE

Compare price, size, and location and count the hidden costs before you make up your mind.

How do I buy it?

The first step is to make an *offer* to the estate agent or the owner. Remember that the price can be cut. Owners invariably ask for as much as they think the market – in this case you – will bear; sometimes even more if they are greedy.

But that does not mean the asking price is the price you should pay. You may have noticed signs of damp, or rot, loose tiles or woodworm holes. All these things can cost quite a lot of money to put right.

Point every defect out to the agent or owner and ask him to deduct something from the price. If you know the rough cost of repairs you will be in an even stronger position. Try to bargain a bit, and remember that estate agents also have a vested interest in keeping prices high because they get paid on a commission basis.

WISEGUIDE

Never pay the price you are asked without counting off the cost of repairs.

How much will buying cost?

Once you agree a price find yourself a good solicitor and start looking for a mortgage. You may be able to get details from your bank manager or solicitor, you may find that the local council has a special mortgage scheme or that the area has its own local building society. Have the house surveyed as a check on your own preliminary investigations to make quite sure that you are not going to be faced with heavy unexpected bills after you have moved in.

After that, purchase should be fairly plain sailing, providing the house has no snags and you can raise the money. Your solicitor will tell you if there are any planning or redevelopment schemes that might affect the house, and about any restrictive covenants that could affect your freedom of use. (It is possible to do without a solicitor, but this is only wise if you know very clearly what you are doing.)

The house becomes yours the moment contracts are exchanged, and you can move in as soon as you have completed purchase – in other words as soon as the seller has been paid.

You can see from the chart that the cost of buying includes quite a few bills. For a start you have to pay the surveyor. Then you have to pay the bill for the mortgage valuation. After that comes your deposit (you can read what that is in the next chapter). Then there are the mortgage guarantee and protection costs (more about them in the next chapter as well), and legal and insurance bills (see chapter 17). You also have to pay the mortgage lender's legal bill.

Most of these amounts are charged according to fixed scales, so you can work them out well in advance. But make sure you remember to have the money ready and waiting, or arrange to borrow it from your bank. (If you plan to pay the costs from the sale of another house your bank manager will probably lend you the money as a *bridging loan*).

Remember that the total buying costs will come to quite a lot more than the cost of the deposit, and that the size of the deposit may prove quite a lot bigger than you expect (see the next chapter on mortgages).

In the example in the chart the total buying costs amount to £791·90. That is £191·90 more than the deposit – equal to 3% of the £6,000 cost of the house. In other words the total buying cost is 13% of the cost of the house. And the chart makes no allowance for any mortgage guarantee or mortgage protection costs you may have to pay, nor insurance, repairs, removals, redecoration or refurnishing costs. These can add a lot more to the total buying bill.

Buying costs for a £6,000 three-bedroom semi		Annual running costs for a £6,000 three-bedroom semi	
Survey	30·00	Mortgage repayments	502·80
10% deposit	600·00	Rates	60·00
Legal costs	105·00	Gas/Electricity	60·00
Valuation fee	13·00	Telephone	40·00
Mortgage legal costs	30·40	Central heating	60·00
Fire insurance	13·50	Maintenance	30·00
	791·90	Repairs	20·00
			772·80
		Monthly cost	64·40

No allowance for mortgage protection, buildings or contents insurance; repairs, removals, redecoration or refurnishing costs.

Based on assumption that owner redecorates and carries out minor repairs.

How much will my house cost to run?

Running costs depend so closely on age, size and condition that generalisations are virtually impossible. But the chart shows you what you might have to pay if you lived in an existing three-bedroom semi-detached house in the South-East close to London.

You will notice that the biggest single item is the cost of re-paying the mortgage at interest rates current on going to press at £502·80 per year. But other running costs then add another £270 – or more than half as much again. If you have a professional decorator to redecorate your house – most need repainting and refurbishing inside and out about every three to five years – you may have to pay much more.

The best way to estimate your running costs in advance is to list all your household expenses, plus any other items you feel you should include, such as car or travel costs, and then add them up. If you are buying a house for the first time, ask relatives or friends. The figure at the end of the list may prove quite a bit bigger than you expected.

WISEGUIDE

Never forget the total demands on your budget if you want to save yourself from unpleasant shocks.

How can I make my house more valuable?

You can increase the value of your house in quite a number of ways, ranging from simple repairs or redecoration to major improvements.

Local authorities can give you a good deal of the cost of any really big schemes. They have the power to grant up to half the cost of any improvements up to a maximum of £1,000 for a house or £1,200 per unit for a house that is being converted into a number of separate dwellings.

Grants can cover anything from installing hot water or a proper lavatory, to the cost of eliminating damp or repairing a roof. But generally speaking they must help make the house habitable for at least the next 30 years.

When you apply for a grant you will have to let the council have details of the work you plan to carry out, with proper plans and estimates from at least three builders, and you may also have to secure planning permission for any major structural improvements (such as building on to the house).

WISEGUIDE

Call on your council if you want to improve your home.

Chapter 6

Finding the Mortgage

Now you know how to buy a house and have chosen it, the problem is where to find the money. This chapter tells you about mortgages; what they are, where you get them, what you can borrow, how you borrow it, and how much it will cost.

Mortgages are long-term investments, loans made by organisations against the security of a house, a flat or even a piece of land. They are generally spread over a fairly long period of time at reasonable rates of interest, and they may well be linked to some form of insurance.

Mortgages are investments

They enable people without the capital to buy a house of their own for cash to buy them on an instalment basis, paying back part of the cost every month in small equal payments.

Because the government allows borrowers to set mortgage interest payments off against tax bills they can sometimes make buying houses with borrowed money even cheaper than buying for cash.

Mortgages are almost always better than cash purchases of houses, even if you have money available. As the value of money falls over the years you are effectively cutting the cost of your house.

WISEGUIDE

Mortgages come from three main sources:

Where do I get a mortgage?

- Councils
- Building Societies
- Insurance Companies

You may also be able to borrow mortgage money from a wider range of lesser lenders, including:

- Relatives and friends
- Employers
- Trust Funds
- Banks

and occasionally even from the person who is selling the house. Some finance companies may lend part of the purchase price on a so-called *second mortgage*.

Councils are often the best mortgage bets. They lend money because they have a duty to make sure people are properly housed.

Councils

Helping you to buy your own home is cheaper than building you a new council house or flat.

More than a thousand councils and local authorities operate their own special mortgage schemes. They lent out more than £155m in 1970.

Because they are more interested in helping borrowers than making a business of mortgages they may lend more easily than other sources. But they may also give priority to special types of borrower.

Against   Their interest rates are sometimes higher than those of building societies.

WISEGUIDE

Council mortgages consider the borrower first, but they can also prove selective in deciding to whom to lend.

Building Societies   These exist to lend money for house purchase. They borrow from the investing public at one rate of interest and relend to the house-buying public at a slightly higher rate. (The difference covers their running costs.)

They form the backbone of the mortgage money market. They lend more than all the other lenders put together – 500 societies lent £1,986m to 540,000 borrowers in 1970.

Against   Because they have investor interests to protect they may hedge loans with quite a few conditions. But average borrowers may find their mortgages easiest to obtain.

They are not always the best medium for the very high salary earner.

WISEGUIDE   Building Society loans can be the best for the average borrower.

Insurance Companies   Generally lend as an extension of their insurance business, and may confine loans to policy holders or prospective insurance customers. But they sometimes lend conventional mortgages as well.

Against   Extra security from insurance cover may make it easier to raise bigger or better loans. But borrowers may have to pay the double cost of mortgage and insurance.

WISEGUIDE   Insurance mortgages may be better if you can afford the extra cost.

Relatives and friends

Borrowing from relatives and friends can be the easiest way of all to raise a mortgage. You may be allowed to name your own terms.

Against

But be wary of borrowing anything without the protection of a properly drafted legal agreement, and make sure the mortgage is tied up in the same ways as if you were borrowing from a complete stranger.

WISEGUIDE

You may be able to name your own terms, but money can lie at the root of many quarrels.

Employers

Many big companies run special mortgage schemes for employees, and terms can prove much more attractive than normal mortgage loans.

Against

Loans may be tied to the job, and borrowers may find themselves tied to the company until the loan is repaid.

WISEGUIDE

Be careful of any hidden strings attached to a loan from your boss.

Trust Funds

These can sometimes prove almost as generous as a family loan, and you may be able to avoid mortgage capital repayments if you stand to benefit from an inheritance under the trust deeds.

Against

They may also be tied up in a good deal of red tape, and securing a loan may mean obtaining the approval of a number of trustees or other potential beneficiaries.

WISEGUIDE

Trust mortgages may help you enjoy future benefits today, but they may also take time and trouble to secure.

Banks

● Banks are not generally very keen to lend on mortgages, preferring to keep their funds for shorter-term investments.

● But they may agree, especially if they are running a campaign to secure new customers and new business.

WISEGUIDE

Bank mortgages tend to be few and far between, but competition can come to your rescue.

Finding the mortgage

Owners

● Owners will sometimes plough back part of the purchase price of the house they are selling as a private mortgage because they consider it a good investment.

● They may also agree to a private mortgage because they think it will help them sell the house more easily, especially if the house is an unlikely prospect for normal mortgages or mortgage money is scarce.

WISEGUIDE

Be cautious if offered a private mortgage and balance the terms and conditions very carefully against the price and state of the house.

Finance Companies

● Some finance companies lend on second mortgages. But be careful, second mortgages take second place to normal mortgages and are generally second-class propositions.

● They generally cost quite a lot more than normal mortgages, they may be hedged about with very strict conditions that can work against your interests.

● But they can sometimes help you out of a tricky situation – and they can prove useful as a source of extra borrowing on an increased value once you have lived in your home for several years (for instance to help pay for a new car).

WISEGUIDE

Scan the terms and conditions of second mortgage offers very carefully before you sign any deals.

What can I borrow?

The size of your mortgage will depend very much on from whom you borrow it. Each type of lender may have certain preferences, both about the people to whom it lends, and the type of house or home that it lends on.

However it will rarely cover the whole purchase price. You saw in the last chapter how you may often have to find a *mortgage deposit* out of your own savings.

This is the difference between the *purchase price* and the amount of the *mortgage loan*.

Cautious

Mortgage lenders tend to be cautious souls, and they are generally very careful to make sure that the value of their *loan* is more than covered by the value of the *security* (your house) that they lend it on.

This means that they start by having the house valued independently of the purchase price. Sometimes the two figures can be the same, or very close together. Sometimes the house can even be worth more than the asking price.

However this is a very rare exception rather than a general

rule. Most house sellers try to get as much as they think a buyer will pay, if not a little more.

The value of the house may then fall some way below the asking price. You will have to pay the difference.

Example You may want to buy a house priced at £6,000. The lender may value it at £5,800. The difference is £200.

Even more Cautious

For the sake of even more safety the lender may restrict the mortgage loan to a proportion of the valuation figure, rather than agree to lend you the full amount.

The proportion may be as low as 66% on an old house, or one that is in a bad condition. It may be as high as 95% – or occasionally even as high as 100% – of the value of a brand-new house.

Example The lender may decide to offer you a loan of 90% of the £5,800 valuation he has placed on your house. That is £5,220. The difference is £580.

What you pay

You will have to pay both the difference of £200 between the purchase price and the lender's valuation, and the £580 difference between the valuation and the amount of mortgage loan that the lender will offer. That makes a total of £780.

You can see from these sums that although the mortgage lender says he is offering you a 90% mortgage, you are not getting 90% of the £6,000 you agreed to pay for the house. If you get 90% of the purchase price you would receive £5,400. In fact the mortgage lender is offering you £5,220. That only equals 87% of the purchase price. The gap between what *you* may call a 90% mortgage and what *he* may call a 90% mortgage is £180.

The same rule applies to nearly all mortgage loans, even the so-called 100% mortgages. You may be very lucky and find a brand-new house where the value is the same as the price. In that case a 100% mortgage could cover the complete purchase cost and save you the cost of a deposit.

However it is more likely that there would still be some slight difference, and that you would have to dig into your savings for a small deposit.

Your mortgage may not cover as much as you think. Make sure you understand all the figures.

WISEGUIDE

What are the conditions?

There are almost as many conditions as there are lenders and borrowers and houses. Mortgage lending is a very personal business. What seems a good security to one lender might attract nothing more than a frown from another. A borrower might be turned away from one lender's office to be received with open arms in another.

However there are two general rules:
- Borrowers have to be steady and thrifty
- Loans are limited by what they can pay

Steady and Thrifty

Every lender will want to know quite a lot about you when you apply for a loan. He may ask for details of your age, income, employment, family, even nationality.

These are all factors which he considers can affect your ability to repay his loan. Borrowers in good, steady jobs are the best mortgage prospects. So are ones who have a good record of past saving (some lenders such as building societies, banks and insurance companies may give preference to borrowers who have saved with them before asking for a loan.)

Borrowers who have less steady employment – for instance people working on commission, or actors – may find it harder to secure a mortgage. Borrowers who have a bad record of rent or debt repayments may find loans very difficult indeed.

The Limits

The lender will want to be sure you can repay his loan. (If you fall behind with payments he can foreclose on the mortgage and sell your house to satisfy his outstanding mortgage debt, but this can get him a bad name).

This means that he will probably limit the total loan to what he feels you can comfortably repay. Most lenders apply two basic rules:

- They limit loans to $2\frac{1}{2}$ – 3 times the borrower's annual income.
- They limit repayments to a quarter of a borrower's monthly earnings.

The final loan figure will be calculated on the basis of the lesser of these two guides. It may also exclude any contribution to family income from working wives (though some lenders make an exception and allow part of a wife's earnings to count).

Monthly repayments are normally based on wages and do not include overtime or other bonus payments, though here again some lenders may make exceptions. Occasionally they may be calculated net of rates.

Can I be a customer?

Mortgage lenders normally lend to anyone who meets their lending rules, providing they like the house he or she wants to buy.

However councils can restrict loans to people living, working or planning to move into their area (though some may bend this rule).

They may also reserve priority for special classes of borrower. These can include people in low income brackets, due to be re-housed because they are homeless or have to move because of redevelopment or slum clearance schemes, residents seeking to move to New Towns, and newlywed couples.

What sort of house?

Councils:
Generally lend on any house or flat, and will also consider lease-holds with more than ten years to run at the end of the proposed mortgage period.

They may also prove more generous in valuing houses, especially older ones, for loan purposes.

Building Societies:
Generally tend to prefer houses built since 1921, though there is a growing trend to accept older properties.

They also prefer houses that fit neatly into the detached-semi-town house classifications outlined in the last chapter.

They may lend on flats, but prefer purpose-built units rather than conversions, and best of all like flats in blocks where a ground landlord is responsible for common services.

Insurance Companies:
Are generally prepared to lend on any house that is in a good state of repair or capable of being put into good repair.

They are often prepared to consider mortages on more expensive houses than other lenders will accept.

Private Loans:
Generally accept any house the borrower wants to buy providing it conforms to loan limit rules imposed by the lender.

Loans from owners selling their houses are naturally confined to one specific property.

How much will I get?

Here again the amount of the loan depends very much on the lender, the borrower, and the house.

However *Councils* can lend up to 100% of valuation, and the valuation may be generous. Loans may be spread over as many as 30–40 years.

Building Societies generally lend slightly less generously than councils. Their loans can range from 70–80% of their valuation of an existing house, and 80–90% of the value of a new house.

However the borrower can also increase the amount of the loan by providing additional security. The most common kind of additional security is a mortgage guarantee (see the mortgage guarantee section) which may enable him to get up to 90% of the value of an existing house and 95% of the value of a new house.

He may also be able to increase the loan amount through a special government-guaranteed 100% option mortgage (see 100% mortgages).

Other forms of security may include money invested in a building society account, a life assurance policy with an accrued surrender value (see also endowment mortgages), a guarantee from a bank or the borrower's employer.

However any employer guarantee would have to come from a well-established company. The borrower may also be able to use a mortgage on another property – for instance his parents' or wife's home – as extra security.

Special cases

Some borrowers may qualify as special cases for mortgage loans because they can buy houses at less than market price, or because they belong to a collective house buying organisation. Examples include:

● Sitting tenants on long leases are often offered a chance to buy their home at very favourable rates because the owner wants to realise what is virtually a frozen asset.

● Leaseholders may be able to purchase their freehold under the terms of the Leasehold Reform Act, and pay much less than the normal market price.

Building and repairs

All normal mortgage lenders will consider advances for new house building and repair work, especially if they feel that the latter will materially increase the value of their security.

However they may also insist that the borrower pays for the site out of his own pocket, and keep the mortgage loan back until building starts. Once building work begins they are likely to insist on approving each stage of the work before they will release loan instalments.

They may also hold back part of a loan if they feel that a house needs repairs to bring it up to its true worth. But they may also agree to increase the amount of a loan once the house has gained in value.

What kind of mortgage is right for me?

The answer to that question depends largely on who you are, how much you earn, and the amount you want to borrow. What you want to buy and the amount you can afford to pay in mortgage are also important.

Basically mortgages fall into three main classes – those that you repay over the loan period, those that are not repaid until the end of the loan, and mortgages that benefit from special government aid.

The first group includes the majority of council and building society mortgages, the second includes all insurance-linked mortgages, and the third includes option mortgages and special 100% mortgages.

Each has its own special attractions, but generally speaking repayment mortgages are the cheapest, insurance-linked mortgages are for the better off, and government-backed mortgages are for people who pay little or no tax.

WISEGUIDE

Look at all the possibilities for a mortgage and choose the one which best suits your circumstances.

Tax Relief

The government allows borrowers to set mortgage interest payments off against tax. This concession can have a major impact on the relative benefit of different types of mortgage depending on your income.

It can make certain types of mortgage effectively cheaper than buying houses for cash, because the real cost of the mortgage after tax relief has been deducted from interest payments can be less than your savings will earn in other forms of investment.

Because it cuts the cost of a mortgage it also means that borrowers can often take on larger mortgage commitments than they could otherwise bear.

Repayment Mortgages

These are by far the most common kind of mortgage and include most council and building society mortgages. The borrower agrees to repay the loan over the loan period, and the lender adds loan and interest together and divides the total into equal monthly instalments.

Because the loan declines over the period the amount of interest also falls. This means that the borrower benefits from maximum tax relief at the outset, with relief decreasing gradually until it virtually vanishes in the last couple of years.

Monthly mortgage repayments

Cost of house	Amount per month over 20 years			Amount per month over 30 years		
	8%	8¼%	8½%	8%	8¼%	8½%
£4,000	33.96	34.60	35.24	29.64	30.32	31.04
£4,500	38.21	38.93	39.65	33.35	34.11	34.92
£5,000	42.45	43.25	44.05	37.05	37.90	38.80
£5,500	46.70	47.58	48.46	40.76	41.69	42.68
£6,000	50.94	51.90	52.86	44.46	45.48	46.56
£6,500	55.19	56.23	57.27	48.17	49.27	50.44

Calendar

The loan amount may cover the full value of the house, but is more commonly limited to a high proportion of the value. The loan is not normally insured and leaves the borrower's widow or heirs with the burden of repayment if he dies before completing repayment.

For Repayment mortgages enable borrowers to buy houses on long-term, low-interest loans repaid in small regular instalments.

Maximum tax relief at the start of the loan enable borrowers on rising salary scales to take on heavier commitments than they might otherwise be able to afford.

Against The loan may not cover the full value of the house and may leave the borrower with a substantial deposit to find.

Because the loan is not insured the burden of repayment falls on the borrower's widow or heirs.

Mortgage Guarantees However the borrower can increase the amount of his loan by providing a mortgage guarantee as extra security.

The cost can be quite low – £4·50 on the extra cover over 20 years, or £5·50 over 25 years – and the premium can normally be added to the mortgage loan for payment purposes.

For Enables the borrower to secure a much larger loan at a fairly low extra cost spread over the mortgage period.

Against The lender may be tempted to keep his basic loan low if he knows the borrower will pay for extra money.

Mortgage Protection The borrower can also protect his widow and heirs against the risk of his dying during the repayment period by taking out mortgage protection cover.

This may also protect him against any failure to maintain re-payments due to sickness or ill-health. The cost will depend on the borrower but is likely to be very low.

For Borrowers protect their widows and heirs against the heavy burdens of mortgage repayment.

Against Mortgage protection is an extra mortgage cost.

Standing Mortgages Standing mortgages are mortgages where the capital remains unpaid – or "stands" – until the end of the loan period. It then has to be repaid in a lump sum.

These form the basis for insurance-linked mortgages, but may also be offered on their own. Because interest is calculated at a maximum rate over the whole loan period they are effectively much more expensive than a normal repayment mortgage.

However consistently high interest also attracts consistently high tax relief.

Standing mortgages are only really attractive if a borrower is seeking low initial payments – low because they only cover interest payments with no capital repayment element – and can hope for capital gain at the end of the loan period.

For instance they might be attractive to a low-income borrow-er who stands to benefit from a future inheritance, or a wealthy man paying a high level of tax who buys a run-down house to improve and resell at a profit.

They may also benefit buyers when the mortgage only forms a small proportion of the price of the house.

For

Repayment of mortgage capital is deferred until the end of the loan period, payments are low, and tax relief is consistently high.

Against

But they are much more expensive than repayment mortgages, and the borrower has to repay the capital as a lump sum.

Joint Income Mortgages

These are a variety of normal repayment mortgage which take the incomes of both husband and wife into consideration for calculating the loan, and phase repayments so that they are highest at the start of the repayment period, and then fall away.

Normally the first three years' payments are calculated on a 15-year mortgage basis, with the remaining payments calculated on a 25-year basis.

They can be very well suited to the needs of young couples who want to pay off as much of their mortgage as possible before they start a family.

For

Young couples can use a joint income mortgage to secure higher loans than normal and repay them faster than normally.

Against

The lender may charge a slightly higher rate of interest than on a normal repayment mortgage.

Escalator Mortgages

These are the reverse of joint income mortgages. Instead of high initial repayments that later fall away, escalator mortgages offer borrowers low initial repayments that rise steadily.

They can be attractive to borrowers who expect their incomes to rise steadily, such as civil servants or professional employees, but the lender may require some proof that the borrower's earnings will rise.

If the rise in income outstrips the rise in repayments the lender may allow the borrower to increase his repayments even further.

For

Steadily rising repayments mean mortgages are repaid faster and interest charges are lower.

Against

But escalator mortgages can prove dangerous if the borrower fails to secure a rise.

Endowment Mortgages

Endowment mortgages link standing mortgages with life insurance cover. The borrower takes out an insurance policy for the amount that he wants to borrow, timed over the loan period, and uses it as additional mortgage loan security.

This means that he has to pay quite a lot more than on a repayment mortgage, because he has to meet the cost of consistently high interest payments and also pay the insurance policy premiums. (The policy insures the mortgage during the loan period and redeems it at the end of the term.)

But he can also secure greater tax relief – both on the higher interest payments, and on 40% of the value of his insurance premiums. The policy may also carry a surrender value after the first year.

For High taxpayers and the young who can benefit from higher tax relief or the lower cost of insurance.

Against More expensive than repayment mortgages and less flexible. Repayments automatically increase and decrease with any changes in mortgage interest rates.

With-Profit Endowment Mortgages With-profit endowment mortgages entitle the borrower to a share of the profits that the insurance companies set aside for their with-profit policy holders.

Premiums are higher than on normal endowment policies, but so is tax relief, and so are the benefits at the end of the loan period.

At the end of a 20-year with-profits endowment mortgage the borrower will receive his house clear of debt and also an attractive cash bonus that may return him double what he has paid out in insurance premiums. The benefits can be even higher over longer term loans.

For Bigger premiums mean even more tax relief, and the policy can secure a very attractive cash bonus at the end of the loan period.

Against More expensive than normal endowment policies and equally inflexible.

Decreasing Endowment This is a variety of endowment policy that covers the balance owing at any point during the mortgage, and normally provides for an agreed capital sum – normally 20% of the policy value – to be paid at the end of the loan period.

It does not usually acquire any surrender value until the first three annual premiums have been paid, and it has been in force for three years.

Varieties of decreasing endowment policy offer mortgage repayment linked to a regular agreed income for the borrower's widow to the end of the repayment period.

For Insures the borrower's mortgage and can yield a useful capital sum or an income for his widow in case of death.

Against As expensive as other types of standing mortgage.

Option Mortgages Option mortgages are a special type of repayment mortgage designed by the government to help borrowers who cannot fully benefit from income tax relief because they pay little or no tax.

Instead of paying normal interest rates on the mortgage loan and claiming tax relief, the borrower forgoes the tax relief and opts for the government subsidy that secures him a lower interest rate.

This is equivalent to a $2\frac{1}{2}\%$ cut in interest at $8\frac{1}{2}\%$, giving an effective cost of 6%, but the rate may vary. It compares with an effective rate of just under 6% to the standard taxpayer.

Attractive to people paying little or no tax, and to people with major tax relief attractions such as small children, dependent relatives, or life insurance policies.

For

Little benefit to standard taxpayers or people who are likely to come on to standard tax rates early in their repayment period.

Against

Endowment Option Mortgages

The benefit to a borrower on an endowment mortgage is a quarter of 1% less than the benefit to a repayment mortgage borrower under the option mortgage scheme.

The subsidy also applies only to mortgage interest payments – the borrower only gains normal tax relief, if any, on his insurance premium payments.

Monthly repayments are slightly lower than on a normal endowment policy and mortgage loans are repaid slightly faster.

For

The borrower has to stay on an option mortgage for five years, despite any subsequent rise in income.

Against

100% Mortgages

These were introduced by the government at the same time as the option mortgage scheme, and combine an option mortgage with a government-guaranteed mortgage guarantee.

They are designed to help people who cannot save or whose savings cannot keep pace with rising house prices. But although they eliminate the need for a deposit -or nearly all of a deposit - they also mean higher repayments.

Eliminate the need for deposits on new houses where a mortgage lender's valuation is the same as the price of the house.

For

They may fall short of the price of an older house, and are automatically tied to an option mortgage.

Against

Savings Schemes

Potential house buyers can make sure of securing an insurance mortgage by joining an insurance company's savings scheme. The scheme provides for them to take out a thirty-year life cover.

After they have paid the first three year's premiums they can borrow up to the full value of the policy without having to disclose any income details. (They may also be able to borrow less after a shorter period at a higher rate of interest.)

Guaranteed mortgages regardless of income or mortgage market trends.

For

House buyers have to make an investment decision sometime before they purchase.

Against

How much will my mortgage cost?

The table on p.77 shows the cost of some comparative mortgages. Generally speaking interest rates are fixed at the beginning of the loan, but many lenders reserve the right to vary them at one to three months' notice. This may be an increase in monthly repayments or a lengthening of the repayment period.

Most lenders will agree to add the cost of any mortgage guarantee or mortgage protection to the mortgage capital for payment, though this carries the disadvantage that the borrower then has to pay additional interest.

Some lenders may also levy a redemption charge equivalent to up to three months' interest on the outstanding balance of the loan if the borrower repays his mortgage before the end of the loan period.

What happens if I miss my payments?

You must tell your lender immediately if you are unlikely to be able to maintain your repayments through sickness, ill-health or any other factor such as temporary unemployment.

Legally he may then have the right to foreclose on his loan and sell your house to pay his debt, but most lenders will try to help by lowering or even temporarily suspending repayments.

However if the lender does foreclose on the mortgage he must repay you any capital that you have paid off, less any expenses he may have incurred as a result of the sale.

The ideal borrower

Last of all, do you match up against the ideal borrower? Are you under 30, working in a steady professional or civil service job, and earning about £2,000 a year. Do you want to buy a new three-bedroom semi-detached house on an estate covered by NHBRC[*]guarantee,close to shops and a mainline station? If you can answer yes to all these questions, you will have no trouble at all in raising a mortgage.

But do not despair if you are not such a paragon. Remember that every lender has his own ideas of what makes a good mortgage prospect. Providing you do not expect too much you should not have any difficulty in finding the money for your new home.

*National House Builders' Registration Council

Chapter 7

Protecting your Home and Possessions

In case your house should be burned down, or seriously damaged in any other way, it needs to be insured. It is up to you to check whether you are responsible for the insurance.

If you rent your house, the position may be as follows:

1. In the case of a short lease the landlord may take out the insurance.
2. If you have a long lease, probably you are made responsible for the insurance.

If you own the house, you will have to pay the premium; if it is mortgaged, the building society may make the arrangements.

● Building societies usually have arrangements with insurance companies, but this does not result in any reduction in premium for you.

● The cost of the insurance may be added to your mortgage repayment. This means you do not have to pay the insurance company separately.

Usually a building society requires you to insure only for the original purchase price of the house. With inflation, this is likely to become out of date quite soon.

Values for insurance

● It is important to keep the insured value up to date, for otherwise any claim may be scaled down by the insurance company.

● Generally, there is no need to insure for the market price of the house. This includes the value of the site, which cannot be destroyed.

● You should insure for the cost of rebuilding the house, to meet the requirements of local authorities, including the removal of debris, and the fees of architects etc.

WISEGUIDE

Keep an eye on your insured value, increasing it regularly, and always leaving yourself a safety margin.

The cost

Most insurance companies have a more or less standard policy to cover the buildings of houses. Generally, the cost is about 12½p per £100 insured.

● On this basis, to insure a house valued at £6,000 will cost £7·50 a year.

What it covers

There is no standard policy for a house, but most insurers give cover which, subject to certain exceptions, includes the following risks:

1. Fire, lightning, explosion, earthquake
2. Bursting of or escape of water or oil from a water or heating installation
3. Damage caused by an aircraft or car crashing into the house
4. Riots or malicious damage
5. Storm or flood
6. Theft.

For burst pipes, storm, flood, riots or malicious damage etc., insurers usually make you pay the first £15 of any claim.

● This is to prevent small claims being made, which would result in higher premiums being charged.

● If you want to be paid these claims in full, the insurance company may agree if you pay an extra £4 a year.

Extra cover

Many insurers cover fixed glass in windows, doors, fanlights and skylights, and also fixed wash basins, baths, sinks and lavatory pans, etc. against breakage.

WISEGUIDE

Make sure that you have a really full policy, and not one for a lower premium giving restricted cover. If the building society arranges the insurance, ask to see a copy of the policy.

Insuring your possessions

It is up to you to insure all your possessions in the house. If the insurance for the house is not arranged through the building society, you may be able to cover them under a separate section of the same policy.

● Here again, the cover provided by companies differs, and not all charge the same premiums.

● If in doubt, go to a reliable insurance broker for advice.

● Ask what extensions are available. You may be able to include virtually all the insurances you need in one document, with one renewal date, and one annual premium.

WISEGUIDE

To include all your insurances in one document is a sensible plan. If the premium is too high for you to meet all at once, the insurance company may have arrangements so that you can spread it over the year.

Cover and cost

Broadly speaking, the cover for the contents of a house is very much the same as for the buildings.

The cost to insure all the contents of the house is about 25p per £100.

● If all your possessions are valued at about £3,000, this will cost £7·50 per annum.

WISEGUIDE

It is virtually impossible to guess how much everything is worth in the house. Much the best plan is to go round with pencil and paper, and to jot down the values for each room. Your possessions are likely to be worth more than you thought!

Restrictions

Most insurers have certain restrictions in their policies. Among the more common are the following:

1. Money and stamps are covered up to a maximum of £50 or 5% of the total sum insured, whichever is less
2. There is no cover for documents, household pets, or motor vehicles
3. The total value of articles of precious metal, jewellery and fur will be treated as being not more than one third of the total sum insured
4. Unless special arrangements are made, certain valuable items may be restricted to 5% of the sum insured
5. Because an item of furniture or furnishing may have had a good deal of wear and tear, the insurers will not necessarily pay the full cost of a new replacement.

Despite the fact that, usually, a deduction is made for wear and tear, some insurers are not making deductions for certain items where they are not more than two years old.

● Typical examples of the above are: furniture, carpets, household appliances, T.V. and radio sets, radiograms, record players and tape recorders.

WISEGUIDE

Anything of particular value should be insured on "all-risks" terms. See the following section.

"All-risks" insurance

Items of particular value, especially those which will be taken out of the house, can be insured on "all-risks" terms. This is specially suitable for: watches, jewellery, furs, etc., and also for particularly valuable items in the house – such as pictures, porcelain, etc.

● Generally, cover applies anywhere in Britain, and sometimes there is an extension for the Continent.

● Not quite *every* eventuality is covered. Among the exclusions are:

1. Breakage of anything brittle (other than jewellery) unless caused by burglars, thieves or fire
2. Damage caused by moth, vermin
3. Gradual deterioration, or wear and tear
4. Mechanical derangement, such as if a watch "goes wrong".

WISEGUIDE

If a watch is dropped on to a hard road, although it may be "mechanically deranged", you can argue that it was caused by accidental external means. The cost of the repairs may well be met by the insurance company.

How to insure

It's a good plan to specify separately everything which you want to insure on "all-risks" terms. Give each item a separate value.

WISEGUIDE

Merely because you have given an item a value, this does not necessarily mean that it will be paid if the item is lost. Much the best plan is for everything to be insured on an "agreed value" basis.

"Agreed values"

Not every insurer will agree values. Seldom is this possible with any item, such as a fur, which may deteriorate in value.

● Values must be agreed at the outset. It is too late after an item has been lost.

● As evidence, produce a recent receipt for anything which you have bought.

● Where you have no receipt, ask a jeweller or other expert for a professional valuation.

WISEGUIDE

After you have specified everything with its value, allocate a lump sum for items which:

1. You have overlooked
2. Are too small in value to specify separately
3. May be acquired during the coming year.

Your clothes

Some insurers will cover clothes and other personal effects on "all-risks" terms.

● You may have to pay, say, the first £5 of any loss.

The cost

The cost of "all-risks" insurance varies widely according to:

1. The type of property insured
2. The value of everything at risk
3. Where you live
4. Your occupation.

If you are a professional entertainer, this insurance will be particularly expensive.

Generally, the rate of premium is highest for those with large amounts at risk (which are particularly attractive to thieves) and also for those who live in London and other large cities, where there is so much crime.

Making a claim

If anything is damaged, lost or destroyed, you should tell the insurers straight away.

● Don't spend any money on repairs or replacements until you have the insurers' permission. The only exception is if temporary repairs are needed to prevent the damage getting worse.

● The insurers may send a member of their own staff or an independent adjuster to negotiate the claim with you.

● If you want to have a professional acting on your behalf, you should employ an assessor.

● The fee of an assessor cannot be included in a claim. This will have to be met from your pocket.

WISEGUIDE

If you have to make a claim, try to keep the cost as low as possible, and co-operate to the full with the insurers. This will speed the settlement, and result in it being more satisfactory for all concerned.

Your liability

In your daily life, at home, and away from it, you could be the cause of a serious accident. In this case, the injured person would have the right to claim damages at law from you. Dependent on the injuries, this could run into many thousands of pounds. Obviously, this is something which you should insure. A normal householder's policy on the buildings of a house covers you in your capacity as owner of the house, and a policy on the contents will cover you for your liability as occupier.

● Generally, the limit of insurance is £100,000 for any one accident.

● It is a condition of the insurance that you must never admit liability to anyone.

WISEGUIDE

Make sure that you are covered not only for your liability in connection with the house, but for all other kinds of liability – although anything in connection with a car must be covered by car insurance.

Other liabilities

Some householders' policies cover other liabilities, but in some cases you have to ask for what is known as Personal Liability Insurance to be added.

● Cover of up to £100,000 may cost only 50p in this way.

Insuring body and limb

You can cover *yourself* against accident.

● A capital sum will be paid in the event of your death, or loss of sight or limbs.

● A weekly benefit can be claimed while you are suffering from temporary total disablement.

● A capital sum will be paid if your disablement is permanent.

● Depending on your occupation, the cost may range from £2·50 per £1,000 insured, upwards.

It may be possible, also, to include cover against sickness.

WISEGUIDE

Remember that this kind of insurance is arranged on an annual basis. The insurers are not obliged to renew it. Or they can impose restrictions or increase the premium at renewal.

Non-cancellable insurance

To overcome that difficulty, different insurances can be arranged on a non-cancellable basis. This means that, once the insurance is in force, the insurers cannot cancel it, irrespective of your health or the number of claims you make.

● In this case, there is no cover for death.

● You will be paid a weekly benefit while you cannot work through sickness or accident.

● This benefit will continue while you are disabled until you are back at work or reach a predetermined age, whichever is earlier. Probably there is no point in being insured for the first few weeks during which you are off work.

● If the claim will not be paid for the first 13 weeks, the annual premium for a man of 35 who wants to claim £20 a week is likely to be less than £25.

WISEGUIDE

Fix up this non-cancellable insurance as early as possible in life. Not only does the premium which you will have to pay increase with age, but you may not be acceptable if you are in poor health.

Other insurances

Other insurances

You can insure almost anything, and it is a good plan to consider how you might be faced with a sudden loss.

● Boats, from a rowing boat to an ocean racer, can be insured. For a sailing dinghy used for racing, the annual premium should be less than £10.

● Horses and ponies can be insured against death, however this is caused. A pony should not cost more than £10 a year to insure against death. You can also insure the cost of veterinary fees.

● A valuable cat or dog can be insured quite cheaply, and, here again, veterinary fees can be insured.

● A wife who is expecting a baby can insure against twins. For cover of £100, the premium may be less than £5, depending on whether there is any history of twins in either family.

● Weddings can be insured. The insurance covers the costs incurred if a wedding has to be called off or postponed. There is cover for the wedding presents, and for bride and bridegroom while on the honeymoon.

● Special policies are available for holidays, so as to cover loss of deposit if you cannot go as planned, mishaps on holiday, loss of money, etc.

● If going on holiday, you can insure against it being washed out by rain. The cost depends on where you are going and the time of year. Average cost is £2 a week for benefits of £5 a day, except the first wet day in any week.

Don't insure for minor losses which you could meet out of your pocket quite easily. But think of any assets of which you could be deprived, or special costs you might have to meet. The chances are, that with the help of a good insurance broker, you will be able to fix up insurance.

WISEGUIDE

Life Assurance

Life assurance should be an essential part of your family financial planning. To begin with it *protects* your family and dependants against the hardships they could suffer if you died unexpectedly. Secondly, it also provides you with a way of *saving* easily, safely, and profitably.

Basically every life assurance policy consists of a contract between an insurance company and a customer covering an agreed sum of money (called the *sum assured*) and period of time (called the *term*). The customer promises to pay the money over the term in regular *premium* instalments. The company pays him if he dies before the term ends, and sometimes when it ends.

The sum assured and the term both depend on the customer. The first can range from a few hundred pounds to many thousands, the second from several years to the rest of the customer's life. The money is safe because most of the insurance companies are huge bodies, with assets totalling many millions of pounds, and are governed by very strict government regulations.

Three main types

There are three basic types of life assurance:

● *Whole life* – you pay premiums for the rest of your life, and the company pays the sum assured to your dependants when you die.

● *Term* – you pay premiums for a fixed number of years. The company pays out the sum assured if you die during the term. It pays nothing if you die after the end of the term.

● *Endowment* – you pay premiums for a fixed number of years. The company pays out if you die during the term, or if you live to the end of the term.

Annuities

Annuities are a form of whole life assurance in reverse. Instead of paying premiums for the rest of your life and collecting an insurance *benefit* on death, as you do with a whole life policy, you pay a cash sum and collect a regular income for the rest of your life. The annuity generally ends when you die.

Protection

The three main types of life assurance include a number of variations that you can read about later in this chapter, for life assurance is so versatile that it covers virtually every benefit need. For instance you can:

● Provide your family with a cash payment or a regular income when you die.

● Arrange for your mortgage to be repaid if you are buying a home.

● Provide money to care for your children and pay for their education.

● Arrange a regular pension for yourself and your wife after you reach retirement age.

● Use your policy to secure you a stake in the stock market, in unit trusts, or in special property funds.

● Use your policy as security for a loan.

Saving

Life assurance can also help you save. For a start the government will help you buy a life assurance policy by allowing you to offset part of your premium payments against tax. This means that you can effectively pay less for your policy – or buy more life assurance for the same amount.

Then you can buy both whole life and endowment policies on a *with*-profits basis. This means that the insurance company will pay you part of the profits that it earns each year, and you may well find your policy worth more than double the original sum assured at the end of the term.

WISEGUIDE

Regular payments make life assurance *easy saving*, with-profit payments make it *profitable saving*, and government supervision and insurance company size make it *safe saving*.

Where do I get life assurance?

You can buy life assurance from three main sources:

● Direct from the company.
● Through an agent.
● Through a broker.

Britain has three types of insurance company:

● *Proprietary companies* have the same sort of structure as normal limited companies, but some of the older ones may have been incorporated under Royal Charter or by special Act of Parliament.

● *Mutual companies* have no share capital. Instead the policy holders are the members and share the profits – and losses. However some mutual companies are limited by guarantee so that no individual member's loss could exceed a pound or two.

● *Mutual indemnity associations* serve particular professions or industries and do not normally sell to the general public.

The Company

Buying life assurance direct from a company can be a good thing if you know that the company offers the best possible rates and rewards, or has a deal specially tailored to your needs. However direct buying may prevent you from sampling the market and finding a better deal somewhere else.

For

Direct buying benefits customers who know what they want and where to find it.

Against

But it also hampers your choice.

Life assurance

The Agent   Insurance agents can be full-time premium collectors calling from door to door to collect hundreds of tiny weekly *industrial insurance* premiums on policies sold to people unable to afford monthly or quarterly payments .

They may also be specially trained salesmen, or professional men such as bank managers, accountants or solicitors who deal with money matters as part of their daily working lives. They can also be businessmen dealing in insurable products such as cars.

They mostly earn their money from commission on sales, and most only work for one company. That means they have a vested interest in selling one company's policies only.

Brokers   Generally speaking an insurance broker is the best insurance adviser. Because he specialises in selling all types of insurance he can pick out the best policy from a dozen different choices, or even tailor a special deal to suit a particular need.

However potential customers should be careful. Anyone can set up in business as an insurance broker, and some are less reputable than others. The best test is membership of one of the professional associations – either the Corporation of Insurance Brokers, or Association of Insurance Brokers.

WISEGUIDE   Choose carefully to buy the best.

What kind of policy for me?   Each of the three main types of life assurance policy – whole life, term and endowment – splits into a number of different policy varieties. But four main varieties are common to all three types:

- *Level term* – where the policy cover stays unchanged throughout its life.

- *Convertible* – where the policyholder has the option to convert into a more valuable policy of the same variety or something completely different.

- *Decreasing* – where the sum assured declines steadily over the term of the policy to vanish at the end.

- *Family income* – where the sum assured is paid out in regular instalments to provide an income instead of being paid as a lump sum.

Each of the three types also has special varieties or attractions of its own, and there are also a number of different types of annuity.

Whole Life   Most whole life policies provide for regular premium payments right up to death. However the prospect of regular premium payments after retirement might prove too much of a burden. *Limited payment policies* enable the policyholder to pay slightly higher premiums until he retires, and then premiums cease.

Decreasing whole life with-profit policies provide whole life cover at much lower cost than normal with-profit policies. The premiums are calculated as if the sum assured decreased over a fixed number of years. However it never actually declines, as the decrease is made up from the with-profit bonus payments. Once the decrease period ends, premiums cease and the policy appreciates rapidly in value.

For

Whole life policies are good buys for men who want to leave their families a little nest egg when they die.

Against

But the policyholder cannot touch the money and the sum assured may be whittled away by inflation.

Term

Term assurance often provides the cheapest form of cover because no benefits are paid if the policyholder survives the term – and it can often be very attractive to young people seeking high cover at low cost.

Decreasing term assurance is often known as *mortgage protection* assurance because mortgage lenders make borrowers insure their lives for the mortgage repayment period on a decreasing term basis. The sum assured equals the loan amount and provides the lender with additional loan security. Some forms of decreasing term assurance provide a special end of term capital bonus in the form of a cash payment or a fully paid-up whole life policy.

For

Term assurance gives the largest amount of cover at the lowest cost.

Against

But the term is limited and generally there is nothing for the policyholder when the assurance expires.

Endowment

With-profit endowment policies are the most popular form of assurance sold in Britain today. They enable the policyholder to save an attractive capital sum that can often be doubled by the addition of with-profit bonuses.

They often form the basis of mortgage loan agreements, with the building society using the endowment policy as additional loan security (see the chapter on mortgages).

They are also the basis of most equity and other *linked contracts* which are discussed in detail later in this chapter. The insurance premiums are partly invested in normal insurance investments, partly in special unit trusts or share or property funds.

Other forms of special endowment policy include *children's* and *educational* policies. Both make attractive gifts for grandparents, godparents, or other close relatives. The policyholder insures against dying before the child, and the policy terminates when the child comes of age with a cash payment or a fully paid up life policy.

Educational policies assure children against the risk of their father dying and failing to pay for their education. The policy is secured on the same basis as a child's policy, with the insurance company undertaking to pay educational bills from an agreed age over an agreed period.

For Endowment policies enable policyholders to accumulate attractive sums of capital that can often amount to double their original investment.

Against But policies linked to stockmarkets or special property funds *may* contain a greater element of risk than conventional endowments.

Annuities Annuities include a certain element of risk. You pay a capital sum to purchase an income which ends when you die (though there are some *guaranteed annuities* which underwrite capital repayment), and you take a chance on dying before you recover your investment – it takes some years, depending on your age before you start to make a profit.

The most common kind is an *immediate annuity*, where the buyer pays a lump sum and starts receiving a regular half-yearly sum six months later. But you can also buy *deferred annuities* on an instalment basis, and some include a cash option.

Then you can protect against future inflation with a *variable annuity*; this is basically a deferred annuity linked to unit trusts in the same way as an equity-linked endowment policy.

Annuities can also be used to provide special *personal pension policies* for self-employed professionals, farmers and other people who fall outside the scope of normal occupational pension schemes. Sometimes the annuitant can take his pension early if he is disabled before reaching retirement age, sometimes he can leave it to his widow or dependants if he dies prematurely. People who do belong to occupational pension schemes can also supplement their pensions by buying endowment policies and having them paid out in the form of annuities.

Other special schemes offer *joint survivorship annuities* for those who want a continuing income if either one dies. The annuity is jointly secured on both lives and normally falls by about a third in the case of a death. Another version of a joint annuity is a *reversionary annuity* for people who want to insure income for a companion if they die. If the purchaser dies first, the companion gets the annuity, but if the companion dies first then the annuity ends.

There are also *minimum annuities* which guarantee a certain minimum annuity income for five years with the option of a cash payment at the end of the period to enable the annuitant to find himself a better deal if annuity rates have risen.

WISEGUIDE

Choose the policy that suits you best, because life assurance has something for everyone.

The amount of cover will depend very much on you and your family needs. You will obviously want to insure your mortgage if you are buying a house, and provide against capital debt payments if you have any hire purchase commitments. Then you may want to provide for the cost of your funeral, for your children's future education, and furnish your wife and family with a steady income to carry them through at least until they are all capable of fending for themselves.

How much should I cover?

That means arranging a combination of capital payment and family income benefit. The best way to calculate your exact needs is to do two sums. The first should add all your outstanding commitments at death, the second should calculate the maximum protection your wife will need in income terms. If you have small children this may equal the present cost of running your home, if you have no children the amount will probably be much less. But make sure you assure your family against any possible unnecessary hardship.

Be sure to cover all the costs of death and protect your family properly.

WISEGUIDE

Once you have paid some of your life assurance premiums, your policy will probably acquire a certain *surrender value* (term assurances tend to be exceptions). This means that you may be able to get part of your premium payments back by cashing in the policy – or else you may be able to use it as security for a loan.

Surrender values and penalties

However the time before your policy acquires this surrender value and the amount the company will pay depend very much on the company and the policy. For instance:

- Most companies insist on your paying premiums for at least two or three years.
- But some policies may acquire a surrender value after the very first premium payment.
- On the other hand some companies may make you wait as long as five years.

The amount is also likely to be quite a lot less than the total amount you have paid in premiums. For instance the company will probably charge you a *penalty* for cashing in. This will include the cost of insuring you, plus the cost of expenses and commissions paid in selling you the policy. (Loan values are likely to be anything from 5–10% lower than surrender values.)

To give you some examples of how surrender values can vary, here are two examples of £1,000 whole life with-profit policies issued by two leading companies:

- *Company A* charges £22.75 a year premiums.

- *Company B* charges £32.10 a year.

	Company A		Company B	
	premiums	surrender value	premiums	surrender value
after 5 years	113.75	46.00	160.50	56.00
after 10 years	227.50	131.00	321.00	135.00
after 15 years	341.25	223.00	481.50	226.00
after 20 years	455.00	320.00	642.00	323.00

You can see from these figures that *Company B* is charging you nearly twice as much each year for your policy, but will only pay you £3 more if you cash it in after 20 years. You will also notice that *Company B* only allows you just over half the value of your total premium payments, whereas *Company A* allows you a much higher proportion.

You can also see that cashing in makes less sense than keeping up your premium payments. Both these policies are with-profits, which means that after 20 years both will be worth a lot more than the total premium payment value.

WISEGUIDE

Find out what you can get before you start to pay and remember that insurance gives better value when you keep up your payments.

How much will it cost?

The cost of life assurance depends very much on the age, health, and sometimes even the employment of the person buying assurance. Younger people pay less than their elders, the healthy pay less than the sick, clerks in safe office jobs pay less than racing drivers or airline pilots.

But taking an average man of 30:

● £1,000 of *level term* assurance over 25 years would cost about £0·20 a month.

● £3,000 of *reducing term* or £10 a month for the balance of 25 years would cost about £0·30 a month.

● £1,000 of *whole life* would cost about £1 a month without-profits, and about £1·50 with-profits (to yield a 90% surrender value at age 65).

● £1,000 of *endowment* would cost about £2·50 over 25 years without-profits, and about £5 a month with-profits.

And at 35 the same man could probably buy:

● About £15,000 of *level term* cover for 20 years for £5 a month.

● About £27,000 of *decreasing term* cover over 20 years for £5 a month.

● About £2,000 a year of *family income benefit* over 20 years for £5 a month.

● About £4,000 of *without-profit whole life* cover for £5 a month (or £2,000 of with-profit that would be worth some £6,000 at the end of a normal life span).

● About £1,500 *without-profit endowment*, or £1,000 with-profit for £5 a month.

Perhaps the best way to organise life assurance is to plan a comprehensive life assurance programme:

For instance a young man of 25 might start with three basic policies:

● A family income benefit policy yielding £10 a week for 25 years costing £21 per year.

● A £5,000 mortgage protection policy decreasing over 25 years costing £10 a year.

● A £1,000 whole life with-profit policy costing £24 per year.

The three policies together would thus give him total cover of £19,000 for £55 a year or just over £1 per week.

When he was ten years older and aged 35 he might then add a £1,500 with-profits endowment policy or an equity-linked plan over 30 years for £56 per year. His cover would now include:

● £1,300 of whole life insurance.
● £4,000 mortgage protection.
● £7,800 income benefit.
● £1,500 endowment.

The four policies would now give him cover totalling £14,600 for £111 a year or just over £2 per week.

Another eight years later, aged 43, he could add a second endowment policy or equity-linked plan also payable on retirement at 65 and worth £1,000 for £52 a year. His cover would now include:

● £1,540 whole life.
● £2,500 mortgage protection.
● £3,640 income benefit.
● £1,860 first endowment.
● £1,000 second endowment.

The five policies would now give him cover totalling £10,540 for £142 per year or less than £3 per week.

At 65 he would retire and pay no more premiums, but in return his house would be free of debt, he would receive £4,510 in cash and he would still have whole life cover worth £2,200. Assuming that he lived to the age of 85 his widow would then receive £2,800.

Count up the cost of insurance and plan well ahead for the future.

Tax relief

You have already seen that the government allows you to offset part of your insurance premiums against tax, effectively making life assurance cheaper. The actual benefit to you is about $15\frac{1}{2}\%$, or £7.75 for every £50 of premiums you pay every year.

There are also other benefits. For a start you pay no tax on any increase in value of a with-profits policy, and nothing on any capital maturity when you retire.

You can also secure attractive tax concessions on annuities that would be beyond your reach if you invested the capital purchase sum and lived on the income (the average annuity returns about $12\frac{1}{2}\%$ a year, against an average of less than 6% for most stock market equities).

But make sure that you take out your life assurance in such a way that the policies are not classed with your estate for estate duty purposes when you die. You can get expert advice on how to steer clear of this pitfall when you buy the assurance (see also chapters 15 and 16).

WISEGUIDE

Life assurance helps keep your savings clear of the tax-collector.

Unit linked assurance

A type of life assurance policy where a part of the premium is invested for you in a unit trust (see chapter 13) has been developed in recent years.

This idea, combining some virtues of both ways of saving, and in particular allowing the usual tax relief on assurance premiums has progressed in leaps and bounds in recent years. There are now more than 100 different policies available and the majority are less than three years old.

An important distinction

It is important to notice that there are two basically different types of unit linked policy. The difference lies in the amount of life assurance cover provided. Keep in mind that the value of the units concerned will fluctuate along with share prices generally.

Where more importance is placed on life assurance:

In these cases only a part of the premiums are invested in units. The remainder is retained by the life assurance company in order to provide the same sort of assurance benefits as the conventional policies discussed earlier in this chapter.

Often the amount invested in units starts off being quite small and builds up gradually over the life of the policy.

The income earned by the policy holder's units is usually retained by the life company and paid out in the form of regular bonuses. These then form a guaranteed part of the policy's value at death or maturity.

There will be a guaranteed minimum value paid out on maturity.

Where more importance is placed on investment in units:

Here the major part of premiums is invested in units. The life company keeps a small proportion (between 5 and 10%) to meet the cost of the life assurance cover.

The life cover in these cases will naturally be less than that of a conventional policy. Usually it consists of the value of the units at the time, plus the amount which the policy holder has still to pay in premiums.

The income earned on the units is usually reinvested in more units on the policy holder's behalf.

When the policy matures it will sometimes have a guaranteed minimum value of the amount paid in in premiums, but sometimes not. (This advantage is, of course, paid for in terms of a higher deduction from premiums.)

The first type of policy is really a variant on the conventional endowment policies. The second type merits further discussion.

How it works

● A policy must be taken out for at least 10 years. During its life premiums must be paid regularly. They may be paid monthly, or in some instances quarterly or annually. (Monthly premiums are in general a good idea since this means that you are investing in units steadily throughout the year.)

● The lowest amount you can pay in premiums varies. £5 per month is normal but sometimes you can pay as little as £1.

● These premiums qualify for the usual tax relief on life assurance premiums (see chapter 16).

● A deduction is made by the life company to cover the cost of life cover. It varies according to the policy and your age when you start the policy. The tax relief normally more than covers it.

● The remainder of the premium is used to buy units either in a normal unit trust or in a unit trust style fund run by the life company itself.

At the end of the life of the policy you get the value of your units (at their bid price) at the time. Sometimes a minimum sum of at least the premiums paid is guaranteed and sometimes not. In the latter case, remember, you could make a loss, though it is not likely.

WISEGUIDE

Do not undertake this type of investment if you may have to withdraw the money in a hurry.

How to find them

The unit trust groups themselves will supply information about the insurance schemes with which they are associated. Some of the big groups have formed their own life assurance companies expressly to run such schemes.

The sources of information on unit trusts indicated on page 150 will also give information on unit linked assurance.

Insurance brokers are taking an increasing interest in this form of life assurance.

If you already have some life assurance, your own company may also provide a unit linked plan.

Points to consider:

The most important distinction between one unit linked policy and another is the unit trust concerned. Many of the larger unit trusts have policies linked to them and some have more than one. In addition, the assurance companies themselves are increasingly setting up their own funds for the purpose.

These work in the same way as a unit trust, but lump sum investors are not accepted. They are not "authorised" unit trusts and so are not subject to the laws detailed in chapter 13. Instead the regulations are the less stringent ones for life assurance funds.

These internal funds have one particular advantage over unit trusts – they do not have to invest exclusively in the stock market. In particular, they can invest in property. This is helpful when the stock market is going through a long-term bad patch.

WISEGUIDE

It is important to select a successful unit trust for your assurance linked scheme.

Variations on a theme

Property linked assurance

Property bonds have established themselves as a new method of investment only very recently. A better name to use is *property linked assurance*, because that is what the schemes are – life assurance policies linked to investment in property in just the same way as the unit linked assurance policies link assurance with investment in unit trusts.

The usual form of property linked policy is a single premium policy or bond – hence the name. This is because the idea was originally devised for the investment of fairly large (£100 or more) sums and the assurance element was included only to enable the companies running the schemes to sell the idea. (The investment in property bars their funds from having "authorised" status.)

The single premiums do not, of course, qualify for tax relief

A Typical Unit Linked Policy

Premiums: £5 and upwards, payable monthly

Age when starting	Amount of premium used to buy units*
17–33	$95\frac{1}{2}\%$
34–36	95%
37–40	$94\frac{1}{2}\%$
41–42	94%
43	$93\frac{1}{2}\%$
44–45	93%

*Remainder of payment is the insurance element

Payment at death

Value of the units acquired so far plus the sum of premiums still to be paid.
A minimum is guaranteed equal to 75% of total premiums payable during the policy's life.

Payment at maturity

Value of units. No guaranteed minimum.

and the life assurance cover is usually little more than the necessary minimum. There are, however, a number of regular premium property linked policies available now.

The schemes work in very much the same way as unit trusts and unit linked policies. The premium or premiums (after a deduction to cover life assurance) buy units in a fund. The fund itself is invested in property – commercial premises rather than housing.

The fund is valued regularly – once a month is the norm. If the value of the property has increased over the period then each unit gets an equal share of the increase. At the end of the life of the policy, its holder gets back the value of his units .

The advantages

● The obvious advantage of these schemes is that they provide the only opportunity for all but the extremely wealthy to invest directly in property, which is currently enjoying a steady rise in value.

● The advantages offered by a unit trust (namely spreading the risk over a number of investments under the direction and administrative management of professionals) are emphasised when the investment concerned is in property.

The disadvantages

● A unit trust fund can be valued precisely every day because each share has a price determined by the stock market. Anybody inspecting the books of a unit trust can tell if the valuation has been done properly. But there is no such objectively determined value for a building held by a property bond fund.

● All the companies concerned employ professional valuers, but they can only make informed guesses. The real value of the property can only be determined when it is sold.

● The other problem posed by property bonds is that property is not as easy to sell as shares. So if a large number of investors suddenly wanted to withdraw their money, the property bond company might be in difficulty. The law which controls insurance company funds does mean that they will have a reasonable part of the fund in some readily available form (bank deposits and so on) to meet such an emergency, but the companies normally reserve the right to delay payment for several months if an emergency crops up.

WISEGUIDE

The property bond companies have been going for far too short a time for any meaningful comparisons to be made of their performance. Their terms, too, are fairly similar. Your main concern in selecting a property bond will therefore be with the standing of the company running it.

Chapter 9

Pensions

Looking after your retirement

Almost everyone in the country is now entitled to a pension of some kind or another. The income that you get when you eventually retire will possibly be made up of three parts:

1. State pension

2. Company pension

3. Income from your own savings and investments.

State pensions

State pensions are paid to all U.K. citizens whether employed, self-employed or non-employed so long as they have paid the necessary National Insurance contributions. As National Insurance has been compulsory for everyone since 1948, there are very few people left who do not qualify for a state pension.

State pensions can be divided into three parts:

1. Flat rate state pension of £6 a week for a single person or £9·70 for a man and wife (rates effective from September 1971)

2. State graduated pension based on the state graduated contributions that you pay on earnings between £9 and £18 a week

3. Supplementary pensions payable on a means tested basis to people who do not have enough to live on. These pensions are the successor of National Assistance.

Flate rate pensions

The flat rate state pension of £6 or £9·70 a week (£312 and £504·40 a year respectively) is paid to people who have paid National Insurance contributions from the age of 18 up to the state retirement ages of 65 for men and 60 for women. People who were over 18 when the present National Insurance scheme was established in 1948 will qualify for full state pensions if they have maintained a full contribution record since 1948 (there is a minimum three-year qualifying period). If you are drawing sickness or unemployment benefit then you are credited with having made the necessary National Insurance contributions during these periods. People who for one reason or another have failed to pay National Insurance contributions during part of the period in which they would normally have been expected to do so (possibly on account of a long period of absence abroad) have their basic state pensions scaled down.

WISEGUIDE

If possible, regard the FLAT RATE STATE PENSION SCHEME as only a basic for your retirement.

State graduated pensions

In addition to your flat rate state pension you may get a small amount of state graduated pension if you have paid state graduated contributions at any time since 1961. The amount that you will get will depend on your earnings and also on whether your company pension scheme was contracted-out of the state graduated scheme or not. Basically you get a state graduated pension of 2½p a week for every £7·50 that you have paid in graduated contributions (men) and £9 (women).

The position has been complicated since 1969 because the Crossman National Insurance Act introduced the principle of making people pay a high level of graduated contributions whether they were contracted-out or not. This principle has been extended in 1971 so that everyone earning more than £18 a week pays a substantial amount of state graduated contributions whether they are contracted-out or not.

The net saving from contracting-out amounts to 27p a week (men) and 31p (women). The amount of state graduated pension that it would be possible to earn by the end of the century even if you pay contributions at the maximum rate for the next three decades is relatively small.

It is not worth spending a lot of time in trying to calculate the amount of pension that you would get from this source. You should however receive a Certificate from The Department of Health and Social Security at regular intervals telling you how many "units" of state graduated pensions you have bought to date. As each unit amounts to 2½p a week or £1·30 a year this should enable you to get a rough picture of how much you can expect from the state.

The government plans to do away with the present state graduated scheme and to replace it by an arrangement that should give you a better return on your money, but you will remain entitled to all the units of graduated pension that you have bought up to the date of the changeover.

WISEGUIDE

THE GRADUATED SCHEME is not particularly important and is likely to be changed soon anyway.

Supplementary benefits

The third element of state pension that it is possible to receive amounts to a topping-up of retirement income to a minimum figure. The supplementary benefit levels amount to £6·30 for a person living alone and £9·95 for a married couple, plus an allowance for rent and rates. The way the scheme works is that if a married couple have only the normal state flat rate pension of £9·70 and they have to pay £3 a week in rent and rates, then they would be entitled to a supplementary pension to bring their basic pension of £9·70 up to £12·95 (i.e. the £9·95 supplementary pension rate plus £3 for rent and rates).

WISEGUIDE

SUPPLEMENTARY BENEFIT PENSIONS must be thought of as a safety net for people who are down on their luck. They should certainly not be regarded as a substitute for saving for one's own retirement.

What you can expect from the state

Flat rate state pensions are likely to be increased every two years in order to keep pace with the rising cost of living so that the amount you eventually receive when you retire should be the equivalent in real terms to the amounts set out in this chapter. Flat rate state pensions have been increased considerably since the present National Insurance scheme started in 1948, having grown from a mere £1·30 for a single person and £2·10 for a man and wife to their present level, increases that have overall been far greater than increases in the cost of living during the same period. The only people who have failed to benefit from these increases are people who have retired abroad. Their state pensions have been frozen at the levels payable when they left the U.K.

When you get the state pensions

State pensions are payable at 65 for men and 60 for women. This means that if you are in a job where you retire earlier you have to live without your state pension up to these ages. Furthermore, in order to get your full state pension when you are eventually entitled to draw it, you will have to pay National Insurance contributions at the non-employed rate. If you defer your retirement after 65 or 60 then you can get a bigger pension when you eventually retire. If however you draw your state pension and continue working then you may find that between ages 65 and 70 (men) and 60 and 65 (women) your state pension is reduced. At present this happens if your earnings are more than £9·50 a week.

You pay for your state pensions partly by your National Insurance stamp, and partly by the graduated contributions. If you are employed, your employer pays about the same amount as you pay yourself. If you are self-employed or non-employed then you have to pay more for your National Insurance stamp because there is no employer to share the cost with you. In addition, you pay a contribution towards the National Insurance scheme in the form of general taxation – about 18% of the total National Insurance budget. The Government plans to make extensive changes to the way in which contributions are levied for National Insurance benefits, and it is probable that the basic stamp will be abolished altogether, being replaced by a wage-related social security tax. This radical overhaul is unlikely to be introduced before April 1974. In the meantime the table on p.111 should give you an indication of the amount that you have to pay according to your current earnings.

WISEGUIDE

Your state pension will provide you with a minimum retirement income only. If you want to enjoy a reasonable standard of living when you retire, then you must either join a good company scheme or save a substantial amount yourself. State pensions are complicated and are likely to cost you a considerable amount in contributions.

Private pension schemes

If you get the chance to join a company pension scheme, do so. The capital value of membership of a good scheme can build up to the equivalent of 7–10 years' pay by the time you retire. And even allowing for inflation your pension rights should preserve their value in real terms (although this is not true of all pension schemes) because your pension is usually geared to your pay at retirement or shortly before retirement. So long therefore as you continue to get wage and salary increases that at least match increases in the cost of living, your pension should be protected against inflation.

The advantages

● Many people think of company pension schemes as a form of savings based only on the contributions that they themselves pay. In fact employers on average pay twice as much into pension schemes as employees, and over a third of all people covered by their employers' schemes pay no contributions at all. Their employers pay everything.

Think of a job that gives you the right to join a pension scheme as a job that brings you additional income on top of whatever you receive in the form of a salary or wage.

Example: If you join a scheme where you pay 5% of your salary in the form of contributions and your employer pays 10%, and your earnings are £40 a week, then you are getting an extra £4 a week from your employer in addition to your wage.

● Not only are you getting an addition to your pay but you will usually find that this addition is worth far more to you after tax than if it were paid straight to you now in cash. An extra £4 a week on your pay would probably be taxed at the standard rate which, allowing for earned income relief, would leave you only £2·88. When this money is paid direct into a pension scheme no tax is deducted, so you would get the benefit of the full £4·00. Whilst this money is in the pension fund together with any contributions that you yourself might have to make it will usually earn interest, dividends and capital gains *free of tax*. As a result, the membership of a pension scheme enables you to earn more money from your job and to get a better return on your investments than you could possibly hope to do on your own.

Not all schemes are identical

● Pension schemes vary widely from company to company. At one extreme schemes guarantee a pension of two-thirds of your final earnings when you retire subject to length of service, with automatic increases after you retire to keep pace with the increasing cost of living, will pay a continuing pension at half rate to your wife if she lives longer than you do, and will provide good benefits for your family if you die young or for you if you should become disabled. Other schemes, however, offer no more than a modest supplement to the basic state pension.

Find out your rights

There are company schemes where you keep your pension rights if you leave to take a job elsewhere while in many other firms you stand to lose everything on change of job, except perhaps a refund of your own contributions, if you have paid contributions, less tax. It is therefore essential that you examine your own company scheme carefully – preferably when you first apply for a job. But if you have not done so already, you should ask for a copy of a booklet setting out your present benefit rights. You should read this booklet carefully until you are sure that you fully understand your rights as well as any of the small print conditions. If you are not sure about any point then you should ask whoever handles pensions in your company for an explanation.

WISEGUIDE

Your rights under a company pension scheme may be worth as much as any other investment that you are ever likely to make, but pension schemes vary tremendously, so look carefully at your own to see if it is any good.

Who can join a private scheme?

The vast majority of employers now have pension schemes but the fact that you work for a firm with a scheme does not necessarily mean that you will be entitled to join it. For example, there are companies that have schemes for staff only and other firms that have schemes for men only. You will also find it common practice for companies to restrict membership of schemes to people who are over 25 and/or who have completed one year's service. There is another sort of restriction on membership, this time imposed by the Inland Revenue. If you are a partner in a firm or run your own business, then you cannot benefit from any pension scheme that you may set up for your own employees. If you are made a director in a company and you own more than 5% of the shares, you will not be allowed to join the company scheme, if the directors between them hold more than 50% of the shares.

Read the rule book

It is therefore essential that when you start work with a company and examine its pension scheme rules you look carefully at the section headed "Eligibility". From this you will find out *whether* you will be allowed to join, and secondly *when* you can join. Some of the exclusions may not matter. For example, if you are not allowed to join the scheme until you are 25, but if all your service before 25 is counted in calculating your pension, then this exclusion will not matter in the least. Nor will it matter if you cannot join the scheme during the first year of service with your employer.

What the law permits

There is a further factor to be taken into account. The maximum pension that the Inland Revenue will allow you is two-thirds of your final pay. Often this two-thirds is built up on the basis of 1/60th of final pay for each year of service. To avoid infringing the Inland Revenue rules your company scheme will limit your maximum years of pensionable service to 40 so that you cannot get a pension of more than 40/60ths final pay. If your retirement age is 65, then there is clearly no point in your joining a pension scheme before you are 25 in order to qualify for two-thirds final pay.

WISEGUIDE

Look carefully at the eligibility section in the Rules of your Employer's Scheme. Find out whether:

(a) You are allowed to join

(b) Age or service restrictions will affect your eventual entitlement to pension.

How to calculate your company pension

How much pension will your firm pay you? If you read your pension scheme booklet you will generally find that your pension is calculated on one of the following ways:

(a) 1/60th, 1/80th or some other fraction of your *final* pay for each year of service

(b) A similar fraction of your *average* pay for each year of service – this may be expressed in the form of a table stating for example that if you earn between £1,500 and £2,000 a year you will get £30 pension for that year

(c) You and your employer pay a fixed amount of contributions and you get whatever pension this money will buy (this is called a money purchase scheme)

(d) A fixed amount of pension is awarded for each year of service no matter how much you earn – this is usually a fairly low amount, and this type of scheme tends to be used for "hourly paid" or "works" employees.

Of these different ways of working out your pension, by far the most satisfactory is the first one which bases your pension on your final pay. Whatever inflation takes place between the year in which you start work and the year in which you eventually retire will be largely offset because your pension will be based on your pre-retirement pay. A common formula for final pay schemes is 1/60th final pay for each year of service giving you two-thirds final pay for 40 years.

• Is your pension based on *all* your pay or merely part of it? Some schemes exclude all bonuses, all overtime and various other additional earnings in calculating your *pensionable* pay. If these various items form a substantial part of your pay – say more than 20% – then a pension which fails to take them into account is not going to enable you to maintain your pre-retirement standard of living once you retire. Usually the Inland Revenue will insist on fluctuating items in your pay packet being averaged over the last three years.

• Look carefully at the definition of your pensionable salary. Some pension schemes make a substantial deduction to allow for the National Insurance scheme pension. This may be a token deduction of £250 or £300 a year from your pay in calculating your pensionable pay, but in other schemes it can be so large as to cut your pension expectations considerably.

Example: some schemes are described as "integrated" schemes. They may promise you a pension of two-thirds final pay *less* your state pension. Suppose you were earning £20. Two-thirds final pay would be £13·34. *If you had to deduct the married man's state pension of £9·70, your company pension would only be worth £3·64 and not £13·34.*

Will your pension be enough to live on? To find this out you must look at the pension formula in your scheme booklet and calculate your expected pension on the basis of your present earnings. Watch carefully for any deductions that may be made from your actual pay in calculating your pensionable pay.

In most company pension schemes the Inland Revenue will not allow your employer to pay you a large tax free capital sum at retirement. The formula that the Inland Revenue hope to make compulsory by 1980 is a maximum capital sum payment of 3/80ths of final pay for each year of service. Quite a number of schemes will allow you to take one-quarter of the capital value of all your retirement benefits in the form of a lump sum. This was the Inland Revenue formula before the 1970 Finance Act.

Many pension schemes promise you a pension of 1/80th of your final pay for each year of service *plus* a capital sum at retirement of 3/80th final pay per year of service. Generally speaking this pension of 1/80th plus the lump sum of 3/80ths has been considered to be the equivalent of a pension of 60ths.

There is an important advantage in being able to take part of your pension rights in the form of a lump sum. Not only is it convenient to have the capital at this time in life, but there is also the tax advantage that if you take the lump sum and then go and buy an annuity with it you pay less tax overall than you would had all your pension been taken in the form of non-commutable pension.

This happens because you pay less tax on the annuity that you would buy with the capital sum you get from your pension scheme at retirement age than the tax you would pay on any direct pension payments from that scheme. This tax advantage means roughly that you can increase the net after tax pension in such circumstances by 30% – if you take the maximum cash sum that your employer allows you to take at normal retirement age.

WISEGUIDE

How much will your employer allow you to take from your pension scheme in the form of lump sum payments at retirement age? Even if you wish to take all your retirement benefit in the form of income you should nevertheless consider taking the maximum possible benefit in the form of a lump sum and using this money to buy an annuity, thereby cutting your tax bill.

Employees' contributions to pension schemes

About a third of all the employees in pension schemes pay no contribution at all. For those who do have to pay, the rates of contributions vary considerably but most people pay between 3% and 6% of pay.

Pay for pension purposes ("pensionable pay") may not be the same as your actual pay because it may exclude bonuses, over-time and even a substantial slice of your wage or salary.

There is a lot of argument about whether it is better to be in a contributory or a non-contributory scheme. Clearly it is better to be in a good scheme even though you have to pay contributions than in a bad scheme where you contribute nothing. For example, if your employer pays 10% of your earnings and you pay 5% into a scheme to get a pension of two-thirds of your final pay you are doing better than if you were in a non-contributory scheme where your employer merely pays 5% of your pay.

The important thing is to assess the total value of your company pension scheme in terms of extra pay and from this gross estimate you then deduct your own contributions. The net result should be thought of as the value to yourself of being in a pension scheme over and above the amounts you receive from your employer in the form of a wage or salary.

WISEGUIDE

About two-thirds of all employees in pension schemes have to pay contributions. A contributory pension scheme is not necessarily worse than a non-contributory scheme. You must consider your own scheme as a whole and then make allowance for the amount you yourself have to pay in contributions.

National Insurance Contributions paid by Employees
(Stamp plus Earnings-related Contributions)

Weekly Earnings	MALE		FEMALE	
	Full Graduated Contributions	Contracted Out	Full Graduated Contributions	Contracted Out
£20	£1.42	£1.15	£1.29	£0.98
£30	£1.85	£1.58	£1.72	£1.41
£42 and over	£2.35	£2.08	£2.22	£1.91

Rates introduced from September 1971

Tax

In most company pension schemes your contributions are treated as an expense for tax purposes. There are some schemes however which give you life assurance relief, i.e. only 2/5ths of your contributions qualify for relief in the same way as premiums to a life assurance policy. The 1970 Finance Act extended expense relief to all pension contributions to schemes approved by the Inland Revenue under the terms of this Act, but it could be some years before all pensions schemes do conform to the conditions laid down in this Act. There are often good tax reasons for not conforming to the 1970 Act unless your company has to.

Points to remember

● All pension schemes have to be approved by the Inland Revenue. If not, any money that your employer pays into the scheme on your behalf will be added to your salary or wage and taxed as if it were your current income even though you never receive this money.

● If you are in a pension scheme that is approved by the Inland Revenue you are likely to receive substantial amounts of money that are not subject to tax, but which would be subject to tax if they were paid to you in the form of a wage or salary.

● Once this money has been paid into a pension scheme it is usually able to chalk up interest, earnings and dividends free of tax, and also capital gains free of tax. As a result you ought to be able to earn a much higher yield on your money through a pension scheme than you could ever hope to earn by investing this sum yourself – without these important tax concessions.

● Remember that when you retire the Inland Revenue will charge you tax on your pension P.A.Y.E. You should also note that you will be charged tax on your state pension even though you are unlikely to have received any tax relief on the contributions that you will have paid towards this state pension.

WISEGUIDE

Tax relief can play a very important part in determining what you get from your company pension scheme. Tax relief is dependent on your company scheme being approved by the Inland Revenue and this approval means that your scheme must be subject to a set of standard Inland Revenue rules.

Pension scheme retirement ages

Most pension schemes have what is described as a normal retirement age. This does not mean that you have to retire at this age because the rules usually allow you to retire earlier or later by agreement with your employer.

The importance of a fixed normal retirement age is that it guarantees you a right to your pension at a given point in time. The state retirement ages are 65 for men and 60 for women. The majority of company pension schemes have adopted these retirement ages but a considerable number of schemes will now start paying men a pension from age 60 and women from age 55. Sometimes these earlier retirement ages are related to the stresses and strains of the particular occupation. For example, the Police pension scheme provides for retirement in the early 50's and many airlines require their pilots to retire at 55. The tendency is for executives to retire at age 60 rather than 65, and many public service employees such as doctors and teachers have the right to retire at 60.

Remember

The earlier your retirement age the more your pension rights are likely to be worth. For example, a pension payable from age 60 is probably worth half as much again as the same pension starting at 65. If you are entitled to a pension of £1,000 a year at age 60, but do not draw it immediately because you are carrying on working then it should increase in value by about 50% by age 65.

WISEGUIDE

Check carefully the age at which you are entitled to retire. Generally speaking the earlier the scheme retirement age, the more your pension rights are worth, but actual benefits may be that much worse if you take them earlier.

Changing jobs

Not everyone expects to stay in the same job up to retirement age and in fact the younger you are the greater your chances of moving to another job. When you take a job and join a company pension scheme one of the first things you must find out is what benefits you will get from this scheme if you leave the firm before you retire.

What to aim for

Ideally, you ought to be able to build up pension rights from a number of different firms if you have a number of jobs and finish up with a total pension more or less equivalent to what you would have received had you stayed in one job all the time.

In practice only about a third of all pensionable jobs allow you to keep your pension rights when you leave. It is however anticipated that legislation will be introduced in the near future to compel all employers to grant what are known as frozen or preserved pensions to employees who leave after a minimum period of service.

Transferable schemes

Keeping your pension rights on change of job means in effect keeping the money that your employer has paid into the pension scheme on your behalf. Where a pension scheme allows you to do this it is normally said to be a transferable scheme and this "transferability" can operate in two ways:

1. A preserved pension based on your salary at the time of leaving and on the number of years you have worked for the firm is paid to you when you eventually retire

2. A lump sum transfer is made to the pension scheme operated by the employer to whom you are moving.

Generally speaking you cannot expect to get a larger pension for your transfer value than you would have received had all this money been left in your original scheme.

A warning

If your pension scheme is contributory then you will usually have the right to take a cash refund of your contributions (less tax) if you leave. However, if you do take this refund you will find that you cannot keep any pension that has been bought by your employer's contributions. This is an Inland Revenue rule and it normally means that it is very much against your interest to take a lump sum refund of your contributions on change of job unless you are desperately hard up for cash.

WISEGUIDE

When you take a job check carefully whether your company scheme will allow you to keep your pension if you leave. Where a scheme allows you to take a cash refund of your own contributions you will normally find that this means throwing away any right to benefit from the money your employer has paid into the scheme.

Widows' pensions

A valuable addition

Some pension schemes provide for a continuing pension to an employee's widow at either one-half or one-third rate, but many do not. As wives are on average younger than their husbands, and as women live longer than men, the right to a continuing widow's pension is a valuable addition to your own pension rights. In schemes which do not give an automatic widow's pension it is usually up to the employee to take a cut in his own pension in order to provide a continuing pension for his wife. What often happens is that an employee will take a cut of say 20%, reducing his own pension from let us say £1,000 a year to

£800 a year. Then if he dies first his wife would get a widow's pension of £400 a year.

Guarantees from your employer

What happens in many schemes is that the employer pays for a guarantee on your pension. This means that if you retire on a pension of say £1,000 a year and you die shortly afterwards then your family should receive a payment or series of payments representing the pension that would be payable for a minimum period of five years or ten years. Most pensions are guaranteed for five years although there are a few schemes that give you a 10-year guarantee.

Avoiding estate duty

These guarantees are often phrased in such a way so that your family avoids having to pay Estate Duty. What happens is that the rules of your scheme would give the Trustees of the scheme power to pay a discretionary amount to your dependants. In practice this discretionary amount would normally be the equivalent of any unpaid instalments of your pension due during the guarantee period of five or ten years.

WISEGUIDE

If your pension scheme provides for a continuing pension to your wife it is worth substantially more than a pension scheme which only pays you a pension. If there is no widow's pension then you must be prepared to give up part of your own pension in order to provide a continuing pension for your wife. Watch the Estate Duty position.

Increases in pension after retirement

However good your pension scheme may be in beating the inflation that takes place during your years at work, you must face up to the fact that inflation is likely to continue after you retire. Some of the really big company pension schemes have been making good the ravages of inflation by increasing pensions to their ex-employees. For employees in small or medium-sized firms it is important to ensure that the employer puts enough money into the pension scheme to provide for automatic increases in pensions after retirement age, even if the firm has ceased to exist by that date.

If inflation is running at about 5% a year after you retire, this means that the purchasing power of your pension will have dropped by about half after 13 years – a man's expectation of life at 65. A guaranteed rate of increase in your pension of 5% per annum will offset this fall in purchasing power. If the rules of your employer's scheme provide for increases in pension at this level, then the value of your pension scheme is effectively increased by between 20% and 30%.

Check to see whether your pension scheme provides for automatic increases in your pension after you retire. If not, and you are working for a large company, or the state, find out whether there has been a good record of pension increases in recent years.

Associated employee benefits

A good scheme will provide a widows' and orphans' pension of anything up to a third of your salary and this is payable, even if you die shortly after joining the firm. There are however a host of widows' and orphans' schemes that pay very poor benefits indeed to the families of employees who die young.

Some bad examples:

● In many of the public service schemes an employee has to do a minimum of 10 years' service before his family are covered by a scheme of this kind and even when this cover is provided it may be expressed as "one third of the *pension earned to date*". This means that if an employee has only been in service for 10 years then all his widow would get would be one-third of the pension that the employee himself could have obtained on the basis of 10 years' service.

● Widows' and orphans' schemes generally do not cover the dependents of women who may join a scheme. Their rights are discussed in more detail later in this chapter.

Lump sums to families

A very large number of employers provide the families of their employees with a lump sum death benefit that may amount to 2 or 3 years' salary or more. Sometimes this lump sum is payable in addition to any widow's and orphans' pension and in other schemes it is the only benefit payable. The tendency in most modern schemes is to make this lump sum payable at the discretion of the Trustees of the scheme and in this way it is unlikely that any Estate Duty would be payable on this lump sum death benefit.

Long term disability schemes

These are often called permanent health schemes and have become increasingly popular in recent years.

Points to watch

● A good disability scheme will give you a guaranteed income for life of approximately two-thirds of the salary you were earning at the time of disablement. Sometimes the formula will be expressed as three-quarters of salary less any benefits that you receive from the National Insurance scheme.

● Most modern disability schemes are designed for the really hard case of permanent disability rather than for short-term illness. It is assumed that the majority of employers will pay their staff employees during at least the first six months of absence and it is therefore common practice for the benefits under the disability scheme to start only after at least six months continuous absence from work.

● The fact that the risk of disability at an early age is low does mean that the cost of insuring this risk is remarkably small.

WISEGUIDE

Widows' and orphans' pension, or lump sum death benefits add considerably to the value of a company pension scheme. Estate Duty is unlikely to be charged on these benefits if the scheme has been set up in the right way.

Women's pension rights

In some companies women can qualify for pensions on the same terms as men. If they have the right to retire at 60 while men have to continue working until 65 women are probably getting a better deal from the scheme than men because they are retiring five years earlier and they will probably live longer.

Some snags

Many women allow themselves to be discriminated against in respect of their pension rights, because they have not looked at these pension rights as part of their pay. In some cases married women have taken the view that there is no point in paying contributions to a pension scheme because the husband will be getting a pension from his job. In practice the husband can only hope to get a pension based on his own salary. If therefore husband and wife are enjoying a standard of living based on two salaries then they should think in terms of two pensions for when they retire – if they are to maintain their present standards. A wife should try to stake a claim for her pension rights even if she only intends to work in a particular firm for a relatively short period of time.

An area where women often lose out is in the provision of cover for dependants. The very term Widows' and Orphans' pension scheme often reflects an employer's view that only men have dependants. There are however a considerable number of women – widows and divorcees with children, single women with aged parents – who need to be covered for dependants' benefits just as much as their male colleagues.

WISEGUIDE

As pension rights are part of pay it is important that women should if possible join a company pension scheme, even if they only intend to work with the firm for a short period. Women only rarely get the opportunity to be covered for dependants' benefits in the same way as men. If they have dependants, they should take out extra (usually cheap) life assurance cover.

If you have no company pension or if you need more

One of the reasons for making a careful check of the benefits payable under your company scheme is to find out where there are gaps and try to fill these gaps. Also, if you are self-employed or work for a firm that has no pension scheme, then you must take steps to provide a pension for yourself out of the savings you can manage to make when you are at work.

There are special statutory provisions that enable the self-employed or people not covered by occupational pension schemes to save out of *untaxed* income. It is important to re-member that this "self-employed" category includes all those people who are prevented by current Inland Revenue regulations from joining their company schemes. This means all the direc-tors who control more than five percent of "director-controlled" companies. (A "director-controlled" company is a company where the directors between them control more than 50% of the shares.) Apart therefore from people who work on their own or are partners in professional firms there are large numbers of director/employees of small and medium sized (and in some cases large) family controlled businesses who must buy their own "self employed" pensions.

For the "self employed" there are special means of putting aside money for your own pension out of untaxed income. From 1971 it is possible to save up to 15% of your relevant income or £1,500, whichever is the lesser, without any tax being levied on this amount. Furthermore, once you have paid this 15% into a special scheme it can earn interest, dividends and capital growth free of tax. You are only taxed PAYE when you event-ually draw the pension that is based on this tax-free saving.

Creating your own pension

● It may be that the weak spot in your scheme is in the cover for your dependants and for this you normally buy private life assurance cover.

● Sometimes you may leave a firm that gives you free life assur-ance of three or four years' salary but find that you have to wait nearly a year in your new firm before you can be covered for anything like the same amount. In such circumstances it is usually a simple matter to arrange temporary life assurance cover from your insurance company or through your broker.

Points to watch

There are special facilities to help you to save for your retire-ment out of untaxed income if you are not able to join a company pension scheme. If your scheme provides poor benefits for your dependants then you should supplement them by means of private life assurance.

WISEGUIDE

Pension schemes are often complicated and you may have difficulty in understanding what exactly is provided or what you ought to do when you are presented with a choice. *For example:*

a) You may be uncertain whether to give up part of your pension to provide a continuing pension for your wife, or

Specialist advice

b) You may be uncertain whether you ought to provide for your wife by means of a completely separate policy.

FIRST – go to your employer

In most cases you will be able to get advice from your employer and it may be that he in turn will refer to the insurance company or to the firm of pension consultants who advise him before giving you an answer.

SECOND – seek outside advice

There may be occasions when you want to turn to somebody right outside your company for advice. If you are changing jobs and you want to compare the pension rights attached to your new job with those that you are giving up under your old job, then the value of a correct unbiased analysis of both schemes can be of considerable value to you. If you are merely analysing your scheme in order to buy additional life assurance you may find that an insurance broker will give the necessary analysis in the knowledge that he may in due course earn commission on any policies that you eventually decide to buy.

What it costs

Where you are not buying any new life assurance yourself it would be unreasonable for you to expect any insurance broker to do this work for nothing. In any event, if you want good advice it will usually pay you to go to a good employee benefit consultant and to pay him a fee, as you would expect to pay to a solicitor or an accountant. This particular branch of pensions advisory service has in the past been provided extensively in the U.S.A. but has not yet been developed to any great extent in the U.K., probably because only a small number of employees have been fully aware of the true value of their pension rights.

WISEGUIDE

If you are in a job and are uncertain about any point in your pension scheme ask your employer. If you are contemplating a change of job, and wish to assess the relative value of pension rights under your existing and your proposed job, then it will pay you to get an expert assessment from an employee benefit consultant.

Chapter 10

Owning a Car

The Real Cost

Set against Britain's total population of 55 million, the figure of 11 million cars on the road, even though it represents a 100% increase in ten years, does not seem staggeringly large. A truer picture emerges when you realise that 12½ million men and 7 million women – virtually half the adult population – possess a car driving licence.

For all of them, motoring is expensive, whatever car they run – that is a fact of modern life. We have lived with the car for 80 years, but it is still one of the most underrated expenses in the family budget.

The harsh reality of motoring today is that it costs nearly £10 a week to run a family car. This total can represent half a family's net income; it may be as much as mortgage payments. Faced with facts like those, most car owners immediately think of the cash they spend getting from one place to another – on petrol, oil, tyres and servicing – but often forget the other half of the story. This only appears when all costs are written down for impartial examination.

If you own a car, it pays and pays handsomely to take a healthy interest in the money it costs. A study of newspaper motoring columns or a glance at the prices of secondhand cars in the local paper, will help you to understand the economic facts of motoring and the ways to cope with them.

Take the same sort of interest in motoring that a financier takes in the City pages – it will earn handsome dividends.

WISEGUIDE

For the city dweller who needs a car only for occasional outings and summer holidays, hiring makes more economic sense than owning a car. At £5 a day, a fortnight's hire fees are only a third of what a year's garaging could cost in a major city.

But if you do decide that the convenience of a car of your own is worth the expense, then the next question must be:

Do I need to own a car, and if so what kind?

If you already own a car, buying a new one may not impose too much additional strain on the family budget. Only one in ten new car sales does not involve a trade-in transaction.

But it is more likely, particularly if it is your first car, that you will buy secondhand. Two out of three of Britain's motorists drive a car they bought secondhand and even some who could

Should the car be new or secondhand?

afford to buy a new car opt for a year-old model, because they feel it has had the snags ironed out. Women, incidentally, prefer to buy brand new.

Having decided whether the car is to be new or secondhand, the next question is:

What type of car?

● The size of your family and the way you are likely to use the car are the first considerations. Large families, complete with a pet dog, are likely to opt for an estate car, a young couple will favour a sports car or coupe, while a middle-aged couple, whose children have grown up, will choose either a more sedate car or one suitable for touring holidays.

● Before setting out to look for a car, shop around for credit – assuming you need it, and most people do. Car dealers can provide finance, but usually more expensively than through your bank or a finance company (see Chapter 3). If you can walk into a showroom with the equivalent of cash in your pocket it gives you strength to negotiate and helps you to resist the temptation to buy a higher-priced model.

● Secondly, shop around for insurance. Use only a reputable company, preferably one you already deal with, or an established insurance broker. A sports model, attractive under the showroom arc lights, becomes less so when you receive the demand for the first year's insurance premium. Study Chapter 11 before deciding.

WISEGUIDE

If you are determined to buy, get your priorities right – decide what kind of car you want, then organise finance and insurance. Do not feel guilty about "shopping around".

How do I buy a car?

Points to watch:
Price is the chief consideration for most car buyers. With a new car the price is reasonably clear-cut but there are still several ways to save money.

1) Look at the "extras". Some manufacturers charge up to £10 for delivery, others do not. Some manufacturers include the cost of seat belts, which are a legal requirement, in the overall price; others charge between £5 and £12, plus a fitting fee of around £3. Number plates are also an "extra". If you are keeping the car for more than two years, take into account the cost of under-body protection.

2) Most medium-sized cars are sold with two kinds of interior trim, one standard and one usually described as "de luxe". De luxe trim can add between £40 and £80 to the cost of the standard car and will include such features as better quality carpets and seats, improved sound-proofing and extra instruments. One

consolation is that when you come to sell the de luxe model it is likely to hold its price better.

3) Then there are luxury "extras" such as radio and aerial, wing mirrors and cigarette lighter – all will add to the final bill, but it will be cheaper than having them fitted later.

4) If you are buying a used car, remember that there are no such things as bargains – dealers, and even private sellers, know what their stock is worth. If a car is offered at substantially below the ruling market rate then there is probably something wrong with it.

5) The greatest attraction of buying a used car is that you do not have to bear the heavy depreciation that most new cars suffer in their early years. In the first year alone this can amount to 20–25%.

6) If you buy a car more than three years old do not expect comfort, noise and vibration levels and acceleration to be as they were when new.

7) Unless you buy a used car with a guarantee from a reputable dealer it is essential to have a used car checked either by a friend with technical knowledge or by one of the motoring organisations, who will charge between £2 and £7, depending on the extent of the inspection.

8) Whether you are buying a new or used car, ask for a test drive. Surprisingly, fewer than half the buyers of new cars bother to test them before they part with hard cash. Yet any reputable dealer will let genuine customers test-drive a new car for at least twenty minutes.

Money talks

You have decided on the car, it looks good, the experts tell you it is good and it's good to drive. Now is the time to talk money.

A main dealer earns a discount of around 18% on a new car. If he is anxious to make the sale, he may well give you 5% off list price. Alternatively, he may offer to fit a radio free, which is roughly the equivalent in retail terms.

Negotiations for a used car will centre round the trade-in price being offered for your car. If it is a straight cash deal – and it is invariably better to sell your own car privately first if you can – then do not be afraid to ask for a substantial reduction of the forecourt price.

When the time comes to pick up the car, check it carefully for scratches or dents. Make sure you have insurance cover, then drive the car down the road and back to see that everything works correctly, check the boot to see that the spare tyre and any tools are inside and make sure you have the logbook, warranty and handbook.

Driving away

The car is yours – ready for the road.

DRIVING
LICENCE

If you are buying a new car go to the "franchised" garage. If it's a used car, go to a reputable dealer. And do not be afraid to bargain with either.

How much will my car cost?

A car begins to lose money the moment it is driven from the dealer's showroom.

Depreciation

As a rule of thumb calculation, a 1,500 cc car worth £1,000 loses about £250 in the first year and a further £50 should be allowed for every 500 cc increase in engine size. A new car will generally lose more than a third of its value in two years and about half in three years.

On a more cheerful note, there has been a change in the past eighteen months. Increases in new model prices combined with depressed sales has meant a boom in the value of one- or two-year-old cars. For the first time in 20 years, owners of certain models have found themselves selling at minimal depreciation and even at a profit.

Standing charges

Standing charges – the costs you incur without going anywhere – are estimated at £250 if the car in your garage is between 1,000 and 1,500 c.c. and nearly half Britain's motorists run this type of family car. Besides depreciation, the other main item in this calculation is a figure representing the income that would have been earned from the capital employed in buying the car had it been invested at 5% tax paid.

Garaging

Other charges are garaging – an allowance is made for extra rates – road tax, driving licence, insurance, the £1·25 Ministry of Transport roadworthiness certificate which all cars three years old and more must have, and your subscription to a motoring organisation.

If all these figures breed a little respect for the car as a family asset, then this exercise in counting the cost will be worthwhile.

Do not be fooled into thinking that the car in your garage is not costing you anything when it is not on the road. Make sure it earns its keep.

Petrol

The main part of a car's running costs is petrol. As a rough guide, small cars do 35–40 miles per gallon, medium family cars 30–35 mpg and larger ones 20–30 mpg. For GT versions deduct 5 mpg.

A money-saving tip is to experiment with the various grades of petrol and see which suits your car. Over half of all car engines in Britain will run perfectly well on 3 star fuel.

Repairs

The next major cost is repairs. When choosing a car, study the servicing intervals – some models have 3,000-mile intervals between servicing, others 6,000. Clutches on some cars take about 2½ hours to replace, others as long as 11 hours. With garage mechanics, wages reaching £3 an hour in London, this is a significant factor.

Servicing

Many motorists run their cars until something goes wrong. This is false economy. Regular servicing, although not necessarily preventing a failure, can frequently detect it in the early stages and prevent more serious damage. A sum of £2–£3 per thousand miles of motoring is a reasonable allowance for servicing.

There are already almost four million car owners who do some or all of their servicing and repairs. This trend has become so popular that the large petrol companies may soon provide workshops on the lines of the several do-it-yourself garages that already exist, where motorists can use equipment in the evenings and weekends.

Other running costs include tyres, oil, batteries and other incidentals. Just occasional car park fees, parking meters, and fines can add £5 a year to the bill.

Total running costs add up to more than 2p a mile, which together with the standing charges means that driving a family car 10,000 miles a year will cost almost 5p a mile.

Setting this estimate against your first year's actual figures will show whether you are running your car efficiently. Over a longer period it will indicate when your car is becoming uneconomical to run.

WISEGUIDE

Keep a notebook in the car glove box and jot down all your out-of-pocket running expenses. That way you don't fool yourself.

Saving money— some tips

1) Motoring costs can be cut by good driving. Forget about wheel-spinning starts, over-revving engines and unnecessary clutch slip. They all cost money.

2) Remember to accelerate smoothly and use top gear as soon as possible. Brake gently and take the correct line into a bend. It all saves petrol.

3) Good driving not only increases your safety but reduces tyre costs. The tread wears almost twice as rapidly at 70 mph as at 45 mph, especially in hot weather or when driving on curved or rough roads.

4) Avoid striking sharp objects such as kerbs, rocks or holes in the road. Cuts and bruises in sidewalls tend to shorten tyre life.

Maintain the tyre pressures recommended by the manufacturer.

WISEGUIDE

Motoring for most of us is still worth every penny it costs. But it is your job to make sure you and your family get the maximum amount of pleasure for the minimum amount of expense. And the best way to start is *to watch those costs*.

Insuring your Car

Some insurance is essential when you buy a car, since this is required by law. Actually, very few people choose to have only the minimum requirement, for this gives very restricted protection, and the majority of motorists choose to have very much wider cover.

A wide variety of insurance companies, together with underwriters at Lloyd's, issue motor policies, but there are some companies which do not take on this business.

Either you can go direct to an insurance company, by walking into its office, or by filling up a coupon from a newspaper, or you can fix up your insurance through an intermediary. These are some of the more usual methods if you do not deal direct with the company:

● Through a full-time agent of an insurance company

● Through somebody acting as an agent on a part-time basis, such as a garage or firm of solicitors

● Through a firm of insurance brokers. These should be able to pick the best company to suit you. If you want to be insured with a syndicate of underwriters at Lloyd's (there are about 30 different syndicates), you will have to deal through a firm of brokers

● Through the Automobile Association or the Royal Automobile Club.

WISEGUIDE

When picking an insurer, take good advice and do not necessarily go for the lowest premium. During the past few years, a number of insurance companies have collapsed, leaving a trail of debts and their policy holders unprotected.

Certificates and Cover Notes

Before you can drive a car, you will need either a permanent certificate of insurance or a temporary cover note. A certificate is issued by the insurers, but a firm of brokers can provide you with a temporary cover note when the insurance is fixed up. This cover note will be only for a limited period, and it is up to you to make sure that you get another, or the permanent certificate, before it expires.

When your insurance expires, the renewal notice will give you 15 days of extra cover. This, however, is very limited. It applies only in the case of the minimum cover required by law, and only provided you intend to renew the policy.

Make sure that you always have in force a current certificate of insurance or a cover note. Have it with you when you are driving, because a policeman or anybody with whom you may be involved in an accident can demand to see it.

Different types of Policy

Act only

The cheapest form of insurance covers only your liability as required by law, that is, for injury to others on the road. It does *not* cover your liability for damage to the property of others, such as cars. You can still be legally liable for this kind of damage, so that it could be very expensive for you if you had to meet a claim for a new car belonging to somebody else, where you were entirely responsible for the accident. Most people have much wider cover, and some insurers will not sell policies which are so restricted.

Third party, Fire and Theft

This insurance includes not only the basic cover required by law, but also applies on private property. You are covered for damage to other people's property (usually, of course, the cars of other motorists). Fire and theft could result in your car being a "write-off", and so it is sensible to have this cover. The additional premium is not likely to be very high.

This may be the widest, best, and most sensible cover which you can obtain for a fairly old car which might not be worth very much.

Comprehensive Insurance

Most cars, especially if comparatively modern, are covered on comprehensive terms. The important point about this insurance is that you are covered for damage to your own car, virtually irrespective of how this occurred. There are several extensions to this kind of policy such as:

● Cover for the loss of or damage to rugs, clothing and personal effects in the car

● Cover for other people driving the car with your knowledge and permission

● Cover for third party liability while you are driving somebody else's car or motor cycle

● Cover of £1,000 or so if you are killed in an accident in the car.

It is up to you to take reasonable precautions to prevent loss or damage. Even so, there are a number of exclusions, such as wear and tear, depreciation, loss of use and mechanical or electrical breakdown, failures or breakages.

Make sure that you have as wide cover as possible. It can be a false economy in the long run to have restricted cover.

The way in which the car may be used will be written into the policy. There are different types of policy, depending on how the car will be used.

● The most usual type of policy covers the car being used for social, domestic and pleasure purposes. Also, it will cover you (as the policy holder) in person using the car in connection with your business or profession.

● A higher premium will be needed to cover social, domestic and pleasure use, together with business use, but excluding commercial travelling and use in connection with the motor trade.

● If commercial travelling is included, an even higher premium will be required. Commercial travelling, generally, is looked upon as any form of soliciting for orders.

WISEGUIDE

Make sure that your policy is wide enough for the use to which the car will be put throughout the year. If you have the restricted form of cover, never allow anyone else to borrow the car for any purpose.

How the premium is calculated

Obviously, the premium for a year's insurance depends on the type of cover required and the use to which the car will be put. Insurers also take into account a number of other factors:

1 Your age and the age of other people likely to drive the car

2 Your driving record

3 Your job

4 The country from which you have come, if you were not brought up in Britain

5 Where the car is normally garaged, and whether it is kept in a garage or left out in the open

6 The make and model of the car

7 The value of the car.

All these aspects are taken into account in arriving at a premium. Two of the basic factors are the area where the car is kept, and the particular model. Insurers divide the country into different rating areas. Central London is the most expensive, and counties such as Devon and Cornwall are among the areas which are most lowly rated. In some cases, the premium for the lowest area may be almost half as much as the premium for a highly rated area.

Almost all cars (except sports cars, which often are rated individually) are divided into a number of different categories. In this way, the number of different premiums is reduced, but it is quite likely that the premium will be increased for young drivers, or anyone with only limited experience of driving.

Insuring your Car

WISEGUIDE

When completing a proposal form for insurance, be certain to give absolutely accurate details, even though you know this will result in a higher premium being charged. Any attempt to cover up any facts can result in the whole policy being declared invalid.

Examples of premium

Premiums have been increased sharply in recent years, because of the much greater cost of claims. Here are a few typical examples of premiums for cars in March 1971, with the actual premium varying according to where the car is kept.

Ford Escort	BLMC 1100	BLMC 1300	Rover 2000
£61 to £38	**£66 to £38**	**£78 to £44**	**£117 to £64**

Reducing your premium

If you are a new or inexperienced driver, the insurers may incorporate an excess in the policy, requiring you to bear the first, say, £25 or £50 of each and every claim.

If they do not insist on this, you can accept an excess voluntarily, and earn a worthwhile discount off the premium. If you have earned a no-claim discount (see next section), probably you would not make a small claim, but would pay the cost from your own pocket, so as not to lose any discount at renewal. Another way of reducing the premium is to restrict the driving either to yourself, or to yourself and/or your wife.

WISEGUIDE

By all means, accept an excess to earn a discount off the premium. Be careful about restricting the driving. With such a restriction, there will be no cover at all if somebody else drives, even in a life and death emergency.

No claim discounts

Few motorists pay the full gross premium, because most have earned a no-claim discount of one kind or another.

● Usually, these discounts build up in value over a number of claim free years, with the maximum discount of, say, 60 or 65% applying after four or five claim-free years.

● There are various safeguards so that, if you make one claim during a year, you do not lose the whole of your discount at renewal. You may just make one or two steps back in the discount scale.

● Some insurers allow a starting bonus of, say, 20%, if you can prove that you have had claim-free driving experience in the past, even if you have not owned a car before. Some insurers quote a specially low premium for experienced claim-free drivers, which is much the same as if the full rate of no-claim discount had been applied. In this case, the occasional odd knock will not affect the premium at the renewal.

Generally, a claim for a broken windscreen does not affect a no-claim discount at renewal. By paying an extra premium, other types of claim may be treated in the same way.

Knock-for-knock agreements

Most motor insurers operate the knock-for-knock agreement between themselves. Their reasons for this are:

1 It cuts down administrative costs and possible litigation for insurers

2 It can speed up the settlement of claims

Under the agreement, when two insured cars have been in collision, each insurance company pays for the damage to the car which it insures, regardless of which driver may have been to blame. It is a condition that the policy on a car must cover the damage risk in full. This agreement can lead to difficulties:

(i) You will not be paid for the amount of any excess under your policy

(ii) You may not be allowed your no-claim discount when the insurance is renewed.

Where you consider that the accident was caused solely by the negligence of the other motorist, you can try to claim for the amount of your excess from him, or from his insurers.

If you are successful, your insurers may take this as proof that you were in no way to blame for the accident, and thus allow your no-claim discount at renewal.

Be persistent in pressing a claim where you think the other motorist was responsible. If you have difficulty, it could be worthwhile to employ a solicitor to write one or two letters on your behalf.

Taking the car abroad

If you take your car abroad, on holiday or on business, you will have to arrange in advance for your policy to be extended, and an extra premium will have to be paid – depending on how long you will be abroad.

Normally, a "green card" will be issued by your insurers.

● This is evidence that the insurance meets the legal requirements in all countries belonging to the green card scheme.

● This scheme operates in virtually the whole of Western Europe, and most of Eastern Europe.

● A green card is not acceptable in many remote and less developed countries. In this case, your insurance company may not extend your policy. A broker should find the best insurer, although sometimes it may be necessary to make insurance arrangements when you arrive in the country.

● Apply for the green card at least three weeks before leaving, telling your insurers
  (i) the dates of the trip
  (ii) the countries to be visited; and those which may have to be crossed in an emergency.

● When you receive the green card, ask everyone who may drive the car abroad to sign it.

How much it costs

Some companies charge £2 for foreign cover for a two- or three-weeks' holiday; others charge £2 or more for each 10 days spent abroad. The cost may vary according to the type of car, and some companies allow the no-claim discount to be deducted from the additional premium.

If you have an accident

With your green card, you should receive from your insurers a list of local offices and agencies which will help you if you are in trouble on the Continent.

WISEGUIDE

If there is an accident in which someone is hurt, or property is damaged, you should report this without delay to the nearest insurance bureau. Its address will be on the green card.

Cover for the journey

Normally, when an insurance policy is extended for the Continent, automatically you will have cover for a sea crossing of 65 hours or less by any recognised route, including hovercraft ferries. Otherwise, an additional premium may have to be paid.

Normally, you are not covered if you take the car by air, but air ferry operators generally make themselves responsible if loss or damage occurs while the car is in their care.

WISEGUIDE

Check the position well in advance, in case your policy needs to be extended.

Extra cover while abroad

There are a variety of extra forms of insurance which you can have for a motoring holiday abroad. Among the costs you can insure are the following:

● Additional expenses for the cost of hiring a car if you are deprived of your own (for more than 24 hours) as a result of accident, breakdown, fire or theft;

● Additional hotel expenses etc. (including the cost of freight and spare parts) which are incurred to speed up repairs;

- Additional transport costs if all the drivers in the party are unable to drive home

- The cost of transporting the car back to your home, or to an approved repairer

- Cover for the substantial customs charges which may be levied if the car is either stolen or completely destroyed by fire or accident while abroad

- Cover for loss of baggage, tickets, travellers' cheques and personal money

- Personal accident insurance

- Extra expenses (including medical costs) if a member of the party is taken ill.

You can meet a lot of unexpected costs on the Continent, and need much wider cover than in this country.

WISEGUIDE

Insurance which you can buy separately

Although the normal comprehensive motor policy gives quite wide cover, there are a variety of additional insurances which can be arranged.

- You can cover personal effects etc. in the car separately, to give a higher limit than under the basic policy. In this case, any claim need not affect your no-claim bonus

- You can insure against a radio in the car being stolen. This means that you need not claim under your main policy, in which case you would forfeit some or all of your no-claim bonus

- You can arrange separate insurance in case the car is stolen or is a "write-off". All too often, there are arguments about the amount paid out under the basic policy. It is possible to insure for up to an extra 25% in this way

- If you are deprived of the use of your car while it is being re-paired after an accident, you may be able to claim from the motorist causing the accident. In case, however, you cannot pin the blame on anyone else, you can insure for the cost of hiring an alternative car. In one or two cases, this is included in the basic policy

- You can insure for the cost of hiring a driver for up to a year if you should be disqualified from driving as a result of a conviction under the drink/driving laws, or for three speeding offences. This should cost less than £10 a year.

Making a claim

If it is necessary to make a claim, the insurers should be told as soon as possible. They will require a claim form to be completed and sent to them.

● Often, an insurance company will not pay for the whole cost of a repair, saying that there has been some "betterment", and the motorist must contribute towards it.

● If the car is a total loss, the insurers will determine the market value immediately before the loss.

● If a car is stolen, the insurers may wait six weeks or so before settling the claim, in case the car is recovered by the police.

WISEGUIDE

Try to arrange for the car to be insured on an "agreed" value basis. In this case, the value of the car is agreed by the insurers at the beginning of each year of insurance. This value is paid without question in the event of a claim for total loss.

What to do after a collision

In the event of a minor collision, there is no need to report it to the police. Nevertheless, write down as much information as possible about the incident so that this can be passed on to your insurers.

WISEGUIDE

Try to catch any independent witnesses before they disappear after an accident. A reliable witness can be a great help in proving that the accident was caused by the negligence of the other motorist.

Chapter 12

Investing on the Stock Exchange

You are ready for investment on the Stock Exchange if you can say yes to the question put in Chapter 2 on savings:

Can I afford to take a risk?

The answer to this one has to be thought out properly. You may be *willing* to take a risk, but that is not quite the same thing. Before you invest in shares you should have covered your basic money needs in three ways:

● You should have sufficient insurance to cover accidents and emergencies, and particularly life assurance (chapter 8).

● You should be owning a house through the medium of a building society or an insurance-linked loan (see chapter 6).

● You should have some money deposited in the savings media discussed elsewhere, which you can withdraw intact whenever you need it (chapter 2).

Just how much you need for this purpose depends on what you yourself calculate. It depends, obviously, on what sort of job you have, what prospects it holds, how many commitments you are likely to face in the near future.

If you can confidently say that you are covered in all these three ways, then you are ready to consider stock exchange investment in stocks and shares. A share is just what it sounds like. When you buy a share you are buying a part of a company.

Can I afford to take a risk?

Do not invest until you have covered your basic financial commitments.

WISEGUIDE

We use the word as a convenient one to mark a difference from saving. Many unscrupulous advertisements appear using the word "investment" as an enticement to subscribe for very risky projects indeed, sometimes outright frauds. This is one extreme to which nobody should go. The Stock Exchange, by and large, offers quite enough opportunity for investment for most people, without going outside it to increase your risk.

Investment is the use of money not only to get a regular income, but also to increase it. One way of increasing it is to make capital gains, which can be cashed and used as income, or allowed to run.

What is investment?

In the savings section we have told you of the various official schemes by which a guaranteed form of capital gain can be made. These are much more generous than they were a few years ago, but they do of course have definite limits. By investment on the stock exchange it is possible to increase the *value* of your money and the *income* which it earns by much more than these schemes offer.

Value and income go together. Capital gains on the stock exchange occur for many different reasons, but at the root of all increases in the capital value of a share is some increase in the income from the company involved: either this increase has been received, or it is expected by investors as a whole. In the long term, therefore, if you end up with more capital this will undoubtedly also mean that your income will be higher.

WISEGUIDE

Be sure you understand the difference between saving and investment before you begin to invest.

Why people invest

For
- The reason for buying shares is that as the nation's growth puts up prices and wages, it also increases the volume of business and therefore the profits made by companies. These higher profits will be distributed, at least in part, in dividends, thus increasing the income of shareholders, and some will be "ploughed back" into plant and machinery to provide for the further development of business. With companies in general, therefore, assets will increase and income will grow as the economy grows.

- Buying shares of a company entitles you to a part of these assets and this income. They are just as much a piece of property as a house or an antique chair. They are, therefore, along with other possessions of this kind, the only way to preserve or enhance the real value of money while inflation continues to reduce it.

- Shares have the advantage over property or "objects" like furniture, in that they are very easily and quickly bought and sold through the Stock Exchange (though there are costs involved which we will come back to later). Their market price can also be checked through the newspapers which record the principal share prices in their columns and, if necessary, by telephone call to the stockbroker who acts for you.

Against
- The first risk is the obvious one: that you will choose a share in a company which hits a bad patch, or which is a bad company right from the start. To minimise this risk, you must never put all your eggs in one basket, however attractive the proposition may seem.

Price	Ch'ge	Div. pence	Yld. %	P/E
11½	+¼	0.8	7.0	9.7
71	−2	4.4	6.2	8.1
79½	−3½	3.8	4.7	14.5
213	−2	9.0	4.2	13.6
466	−24	13.6	2.9	19.3
94	−6	3.9g	4.1	13.4
68½	−1½	4.0	5.8	11.0
58	−4	3.3	5.7	10.8
260	...	7.5	2.9	13.9
59	+3	3.8	6.4	11.2
93	−1½	4.8	5.1	14.7
402	−6	10.6	2.6	27.8
89	−1½	2.1	2.4	15.9
120	+4	6.3n	5.2	9.3
285	+10	8.5	3.0	14.0
80	...	3.3	4.1	15.3
63	−5	4.0	6.3	10.5
23½	+3½	0.6	2.7	3.7
63	+6	2.6	4.1	9.8
46	...	3.1	6.7	15.3
237	+1			

• The second risk is that, even if you buy shares which prove as good as the average, you may find yourself having to sell them at a time when the whole stock market is depressed for one reason or another. Over the last twenty years, for example, stock-market trends as measured by the *Financial Times* Ordinary share index which is made up of shares in 30 leading companies, has moved broadly upwards, but over any limited period of time it might well have risen very little or even fallen. Our table shows when the index was at its highest and lowest in each of the years from 1951 to date.

Stockmarket Fluctuations

Highs and lows of the *Financial Times* Ordinary share index.

Year	Index High	Date	Index Low	Date	Year	Index High	Date	Index Low	Date
1951	140.4	13/6	115.5	2/1	1962	310.2	19/1	252.8	25/6
1952	121.5	1/1	103.1	4/6	1963	348.4	31/12	279.6	28/1
1953	131.5	4/11	113.9	20/5	1964	377.8	1/10	322.6	3/2
1954	184.0	31/12	131.1	1/1	1965	359.1	3/5	313.8	29/7
1955	223.9	21/7	175.7	15/3	1966	374.2	16/6	284.2	26/8
1956	203.5	3/1	161.5	29/11	1967	420.7	16/11	308.6	28/2
1957	207.6	9/7	159.0	5/11	1968	521.9	19/9	385.0	2/1
1958	225.5	31/12	154.4	25/2	1969	520.1	15/1	357.4	28/7
1959	338.7	30/12	212.8	30/1	1970	423.4	14/1	315.6	15/6
1960	342.9	4/1	293.4	9/12	1971*	352.2	30/3	305.3	2/3
1961	365.7	15/5	284.7	16/10	*to April 13.				

Do not invest if you may need your money suddenly when stock-market prices may be low.

WISEGUIDE

Unless you take the time and trouble to study investment in depth, you must seek advice before plunging into the stock-market. You need guidance on what shares to buy and on the timing of your purchases.

Advice on investment is essential

In this, as in other financial matters, your bank manager is a good start. He may not know much about the stock market as an individual, but he will be in contact with others who can help you more directly. He will very probably have dealt with stockbrokers in the course of his duties and he may be able to introduce you to a suitable broking firm. He may also help in your choice of shares.

Your bank manager may help

Where else can you find out about stockbrokers?

You may also get a list of stockbrokers who are willing to take on small investors by writing to the London Stock Exchange, or your nearest regional stock exchange. Brokers are not allowed to advertise. In the future this rule may be relaxed and you may therefore occasionally see a firm's name in the financial press.

But bear in mind that a stockbroker is not necessarily equipped to give detailed advice to a beginner in investment. If you have only a small amount to invest, he cannot afford to spare too much time on your affairs. So it is essential to have enough sources of advice to check one against the other. Don't be afraid to ask. And study the chapter on unit trusts (Chapter 13) before you think of buying individual shares.

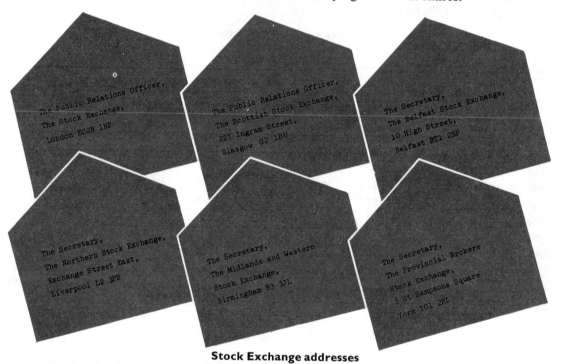

The Public Relations Officer,
The Stock Exchange,
London EC2N 1HP

The Public Relations Officer,
The Scottish Stock Exchange,
227 Ingram Street,
Glasgow G2 1BU

The Secretary,
The Belfast Stock Exchange,
10 High Street,
Belfast BT1 2BP

The Secretary,
The Northern Stock Exchange,
Exchange Street East,
Liverpool L2 3PB

The Secretary,
The Midlands and Western
Stock Exchange,
Birmingham B3 3JL

The Secretary,
The Provincial Brokers
Stock Exchange,
3 St Sampsons Square
York YO1 2RL

Stock Exchange addresses

Learning about investment

Experience, as in so many other matters, can only come with time. If you are sufficiently keen to "go it alone", you can start with one or other of the books on investment which have been published in recent years. The financial columns of the press are useful sources of everyday company news and of background material. Most newspapers maintain an inquiry bureau which will answer specific questions.

How thorough does knowledge have to be?

The more you can learn about companies the better: for example, it would pay to know something about company accounts. The main thing is to acquire sufficient background to check the advice given to you and the comments which you read in the press. It can be great fun to find out about shares: if it becomes a strain, the simple answer is to invest in unit trusts (which are dealt with later).

WISEGUIDE

A little knowledge is a dangerous thing: you cannot learn too much about your investments.

Different kinds of stock exchange investments

A. Equity Shares

The "shares" we have so far referred to are the sort which represent ownership of a piece of a company. They are referred to generally as "equity", because of this right of ownership: and the most common type of equity are officially known as Ordinary shares. Sometimes these are called Ordinary "stock", or "stock units", but there is no real difference. They all have what is called a "par value". This may theoretically be any value, but it is often £1 or, more usually nowadays, 25p.

The par value has no real significance except that company dividends and earnings (that is, the total net profit that could be distributed in dividends) are often expressed as a percentage of the nominal value. But nowadays, dividends are frequently declared in actual cash amounts per share.

For example: Company A with Ordinary shares of nominal value £1 may declare a dividend of 20%, or 20p. Company B with Ordinary shares of nominal value 25p, may also declare a dividend of 20%, or 5p.

The important value of a share is its *market value*, because if you buy Company A's shares you will get 20% on your money if they also cost £1 in the market. Unless the company is a bad risk, they will undoubtedly cost more. If they cost £2 each, for example, you would get 10% on your money. At £4 each, you would get a 5% "yield", as the return on the money invested is called.

$$\frac{\text{Par value} \times \text{dividend}}{\text{share price}}$$

How to work out a yield

For example, a £1 share standing at a market price of £1·50 paying a 9% dividend:

$$\frac{100\text{p} \times 9}{£1·50} = 6\%$$

Yields can be expressed in figures, 6%, or in money, £6%. This £6 represents the actual return on every £100 you invest. In other words it is just like the interest in saving, but it fluctuates as share prices move up and down.

It is the market value of a share which counts, not its nominal value.

WISEGUIDE

Non-voting shares

Ordinary shares represent a piece of the company. They are entitled to a share in the company's profits and assets. But the legal rights on different shares may vary. Some have no votes in a general meeting of the company, and these are usually known as Non-Voting or "A" Ordinary. They may be quoted alongside the Ordinary (voting) shares of the same company. There are several well-known examples of non-voting Ordinary shares, J. Lyons and Great Universal Stores amongst them.

For Non-Voting Ordinary shares are often priced lower than the Ordinary shares in the same company, where they are both quoted in the stockmarket. In a well run successful company, Non-Voting Ordinary shares can still be a good investment and offer a higher return than voting shares.

Against The disadvantage of this type of share is that if the company gets into difficulties, you have no say in what can be done about it. If a takeover bid is made for such a company, the bidder may not need to offer as high a price to a Non-Voting shareholder. What he is after is the vital voting power which will give him control of the company.

Deferred shares There are other varieties of equity share, amongst which are "Deferred" or "Deferred Ordinary", where the rights to dividends or the claim on company assets is restricted in certain specific ways. They are comparatively rare.

WISEGUIDE

If you are buying equity stocks, be sure you know exactly what you are buying.

B. Preference Shares These are not the same as equities. They are "fixed-interest", entitled to a certain payment each year and no more. Since they are quoted on the stock market, the price may vary, and so will the "yield" at any particular date. Thus, a Preference share of £1 nominal value, entitled to a fixed 6% dividend, may be worth only 60p in the market. The "yield" on this would be 10%.

Preference shares are part of a company's "capital", like ordinary shares. Dividends must be paid on them before the directors consider what dividends to pay on the Ordinary capital. Some of them, called Cumulative Preference, are entitled to receive all the arrears of dividends, if the company has failed to make a payment in a previous year or years. But Preference shares are just as risky as Ordinary if a company fails completely, because although they have "preference" over Ordinary shares, they have no legal status as debtors.

C. Debentures and Loans These are in fact debts of the company to the persons who hold them. They are not shares, but "stock", and are usually quoted in £100 nominal amounts. Interest is paid on them, normally twice a year. They may be "secured" on specific assets of the company, just as a building society mortgage is on your house (Debentures), or they may have a more general security, or they may have no security at all (Loans). But they all have prior claims on the company over preference and ordinary capital.

They can be bought and sold like shares.

Debentures and loans, even in very sound and safe companies, offer a high return. But unlike bank or other deposits they are subject to price fluctuations. If the general level of interest rates rises, the market price will fall to keep the "yield" in adjustment. This is what has happened over recent years. If the level of interest rates falls, of course, the market price will rise.

Debentures and loans are the most secure investments followed by Preference shares, Ordinary voting shares and finally non-voting shares.

WISEGUIDE

Gilt-edged stocks

These are the debts of the British Government to private individuals who invest in them. There are more than 50 different kinds of gilt-edged stock quoted: their value runs into thousands of millions of pounds.

The Government uses the gilt-edged market as one of its sources of money to run the country, and to influence the economy by its actions in the market. It may, for instance, buy large amounts of gilt-edged stock for its own account, which would tend to put market prices up and would also leave money in the hands of the private investors who had sold to it. The Government buys and sells through its own broker. His dealings are very discreet, so that no investor ever consciously "sells to the Government". The effect, however, is the same.

The Government may, on the other hand, sell gilt-edged which, on a sufficient scale, will do the reverse. It is obvious that nobody can be compelled to buy stock from the Government. But sometimes the many private investors in gilt-edged decide that prices are going to rise, and this mass movement enables the Government to get rid of some of its own holdings, to keep prices from rising too rapidly.

Four types of government stock

Gilt-edged stock is very easily bought and sold (the costs of dealing are very low, as we show later). It is dealt in by units of £100 nominal value: there are four types of stock:

a) *Short dated:* this means that the stock is to be "redeemed", or paid up, within five years from purchase.

b) *Medium dated:* this is stock redeemable from five up to ten years from purchase.

c) *Long dated:* stock redeemable after fifteen years, and over thirty years in some cases,

d) *"Irredeemable"*: this means what it says, without any date for repayment.

The choice in gilt-edged investment

Obviously, you can invest in gilt-edged stock just for the income. (Interest on some stocks is paid without deduction of income tax at standard rate, which is helpful to people who pay little or no tax.) The risk here is of market fluctuations.

However, you can eliminate the risk if you are prepared to keep the stock until it is redeemed. You will then be paid at par (£100 per stock). There is no capital gains tax on the profit you make on this, either (see chapter 16 on taxation).

The disadvantage here is that the nearer the repayment date (and thus the greater the convenience of holding the stock) the lower the yield on the stock tends to be, and the smaller is the "guaranteed" capital profit. Only if you are prepared to risk fluctuations in price, or hold longer-dated stock, can you expect the higher returns.

"Redemption yields"

Gilt-edged stock gives a guaranteed capital return if you keep it to redemption. So as well as the actual income yield, there is a bit extra each year which finally appears at the end, as it were. Therefore, investors in gilt-edged look at this as though it were combined with the interest (or "flat") yield. When this extra is added, it forms what is known as the "redemption yield". This method of measurement is also applied to Debentures and Loans.

So you don't get the full redemption yield unless you stick it out to the end, but if you do survive the course it is as though you had simply received the redemption rate and just got your money back.

Examples of redemption yields at a recent date can be seen below, compared with Ordinary and Preference yields. But remember that the yield on Ordinary shares is only the result of the current level of dividends paid by the company in question. The risk with Ordinary dividends is that they may fall, but over a reasonable period of time, the expectation is that they will rise. So an Ordinary yield is not the "same animal" as a fixed-interest yield. *It allows for actual growth of income.*

This is why most Ordinary yields are lower than those on fixed-interest stock. Some Ordinary yields, however, are not so low. You may notice some of these in the table. This may be because the profits of the company in question are not expected to progress much, if at all in the foreseeable future, or because there is an actual fear of a dividend cut.

WISEGUIDE

When buying Government stocks, be sure exactly what kind of stock you are buying, and be clear of the difference between a redemption yield and a running yield on your investment.

How much does it cost to invest?

Stockbrokers buy and sell shares for you, charging a commission on their services. There are also two other costs: "ad valorem" transfer stamp duty on purchases only, and contract stamp.

Commission Charges

Some Examples of Yields on Investments
(at April 7, 1971).

ORDINARY SHARES	Market Price	Current Dividend %	Yield %
Barclays Bank £1 shares	433p	16	3.7
Bass, Charrington 25p shares	115p	17½	3.8
I.C.I. £1 shares	255p	13¾	5.4
Lyons £1 'A' shares	440p	12.1	2.7
News of the World 25p shares	130p	37½	7.2
Associated Paper 25p shares	16p	8	12.9
Consolidated Gold Fields 25p	225p	29.2	3.2

PREFERENCE SHARES	Market Price	Fixed Dividend %	Yield %
Cadbury-Schweppes £1	50p	5	10.3
Whitbread £1	67p	7	10.4

DEBENTURE STOCKS	Redemption date	Market Price	Interest Rate %	Flat Yield %	Redemption Yield %
Company					
Unilever	1975	£80½	3¾%	4.7	9.3
Tate and Lyle	1985	£65½	5½%	8.7	10.4
Watney Mann	1995	£105½	10½	10.0	10.0

GILT-EDGED STOCKS	Redemption Date	Market Price	Interest Rate %	Flat Yield %	Redemption Yield %
Stock					
Conversion 5%	1971	£99¾	5	5.0	5.7
Treasury 6½%	1976	£96½	6½	6.8	7.5
Treasury 8¾%	1997	£94¾	8¾	9.3	9.4
War Loan 3½%	Undated	£39	3½	9.3	—

Commission charges

The brokers commission is the biggest item. It is usually a minimum of about 1·25% on shares, provided that the value of the shares bought or sold is over £320. If the "bargain", as it is called, is over £100 but below £320, the minimum charge is £4. If the bargain is even smaller, between £10 and £100, the minimum charge is £2.

Points to watch

● The £4 minimum works out at almost 4% on orders of just over £100, and the £2 minimum can be even higher on very small transactions. So buying small amounts of shares is expensive.

● Commission on registered Debentures, Loans, etc., is less, at 0·75% on the first £5,000, reducing on higher amounts.

● Commission on gilt-edged stock, and various other types of stock, such as Local Authority and Public Board Stocks, is lower still. It is 0·625% on the first £2,000, 0·2% on the next £12,000, and then lower still. This is on stocks with at least ten years to go before redemption. For shorter dates, there are slightly different charges.

Transfer stamp duty on purchases This is at a rate of 1 %, going up in steps, so that it can be a little more on actual value. It is not levied on gilt-edged stocks. Nor is it levied on "new issues" of shares or debentures. (This is when the shares etc., are not yet quoted as such, but in the form of "allotment letters".)

Contract stamp This is a very small charge which is in fact nothing for a purchase worth less than £100.

WISEGUIDE Total costs on share bargains come to 2·25 % for purchases over £320 and under £5,000. Below this, the cost can more than double. Gilt-edged bargains cost very much less, and certain stocks can be purchased through the Post Office for even lower cost.

How are shares bought and sold? ● Once you have been accepted as a client by a stockbroker, you may if you wish simply telephone him with your order.
● You can act through your bank, if this is more convenient.
You must say what shares you want to buy (or sell) and how many of them. You can also (indeed it is sensible to do so) specify what price you are prepared to pay (or take). But this must of course be a reasonable one. If when buying you want a price so low that the shares cannot be obtained, the exercise is pointless.

If you want to buy 200 £1 Ordinary Shares of Jones and Co., which you saw in the *Financial Times* price lists were 300p the day before, you should ask your broker for a current price first. The shares may have gone up or down since the day before. Then having got the price, you must decide whether you are satisfied with this. If you are, there is no harm in ordering the shares at that price. If you think it could go lower, specify a price above which you will not buy. Your broker will know whether your lower price is likely to be unreasonable or not. Take his advice on this. But do not simply ask for shares at any price, unless you have reason to think they are going to continue to rise.

WISEGUIDE Ask, and take, advice from your stockbroker; you are paying for his services.

How the shares are bought You can ask your broker to buy shares at any time during normal office hours. But the Stock Exchange is officially open only from 9.30 a.m. to 3.30 p.m. (although dealing does go on "after hours" by telephone).

When you have definitely placed your order, the broker will contact his "dealer" on the Stock Exchange Floor, who will try to get your shares on the terms for which you ask. He buys them from one or other of the "jobbers" on the Stock Exchange. These are the various people who actually hold "supplies" of the shares and who balance out the demand and the supply of them. To "balance their books" in each share they have to vary the price at which they "offer" or "bid", so as to attract shares on to their books when they are running out, or to sell them when they have too many.

What a "quotation" is

To cover their costs, they make the "offer" price (that is, the price at which you are buying) slightly higher than the "bid" (selling) price at any one time. This is called a "quotation". For example, your shares which are listed as 300p would have been the "middle" of a quotation of, say, 298p and 302p. If you subsequently bought at 300p, this would actually mean that the quotation had gone down, to say 296p to 300p, a middle of 298p.

The contract note

If your broker is successful in buying the shares, he will make out a "contract note" and send it to you, frequently on the same day. This will record the deal, with the price and the total cost, including the commission, etc. It is important to keep this, because it is a record for your own reference and for capital gains tax purposes.

Learn as much as you can; your stockbroker is a busy man and will serve you better if you do not ask pointless questions.

WISEGUIDE

When you pay: the Stock Exchange "Account"

You do not have to pay immediately. The Stock Exchange operates on a series of "accounts", which are normally of two weeks' duration, running from Monday until the second Friday. Any shares you buy and sell within this period are recorded by your broker, who only sends you the record and the bill for the balance. So you could theoretically buy and sell within this period the same shares at the same price and only get a bill for commission, etc., at the end of it. If you lost on the deal you would pay more, or if you gained the broker would send *you* a cheque.

The transaction has to be paid for by "Account day" (or "settlement day") which is usually a Tuesday, eleven days after the last day of the account period. You must do this because that is when your broker has to pay the jobber (and when every Stock Exchange firm balances up with every other). The table below shows when the accounts occur in the last few weeks of 1971. Notice the date for "new time dealings". This is a special concessionary period, technically within one account, during which if you wish (there is an extra charge) you can deal as though in the following account.

When do you own the shares?

First Day of Dealings

1971 NOVEMBER 1971

Sun		7	14	21	28
Mon	1	8	15	22	29
Tue	2	9	16	23	30
Wed	3	10	17	24	
Thu	4	11	18	25	
Fri	5	12	19	26	
Sat	6	13	20	27	

'New time' Dealings

Last Day of Dealings

1971 DECEMBER 1971

Sun		5	12	19	26
Mon		6	13	20	27
Tue		7	14	21	28
Wed	1				

Account Day

Taxes on investments

(see also Chapter 16 on taxation)

You own the shares from the time of the deal in the Stock Exchange, and your contract note is proof of your purchase. But not until the account is settled will your broker take action to put you on the share register of the company whose shares you have bought. He will see to it that a transfer of registered shares is made in your favour, and he will inform the company's registrar, who in turn will send you a share certificate. This final stage may take some time, many weeks in certain instances.

From the time you buy them you own the rights to dividends (and anything else that is going) on the shares. But until you are registered, the former owner will be the one who is sent these. Between them, the brokers involved will see to it that you eventually get any dividend that starts off in the wrong direction. However, you should keep an eye on what is happening in this connection.

If you want dividends sent straight to your bank, you should ask the company registrar to do this for you.

Selling your shares is much the same as buying them, so far as the "machinery" and broker's commission are concerned, but you pay no transfer stamp duty. You will receive a transfer form to sign, because you are the registered owner, and you return the share certificate with the transfer form to your broker.

● *Income Tax*. When you receive dividends and interest (except for interest on some Gilt-edged Stock through the Post Office) you will get it minus Income Tax at the standard rate (currently 38·75%). If you don't pay income tax, you can reclaim it from the Inland Revenue. If you pay surtax, you will be charged for this separately in due course.

● *Capital Gains Tax*. If you sell shares and make a capital gain on them, you will have to pay capital gains tax. If you have made gains and losses over the year, you are of course only taxed on the net gain, if any. You can also "carry forward" any losses and deduct them from gains "realised" in subsequent years. Your net gains will also of course be calculated after your expenses of buying and selling.

● You need not record capital gains you make in any one year if the total amount of your *sales* is no more than £500. If you can, therefore, it will pay you to defer selling more than this amount in any one year (unless it is such a huge amount that you can't wait to "spread it out"). You do not have to pay capital gains tax on gains of any size on Gilt-edged stock, unless you sell it within a year of buying it.

● The flat rate of capital gains tax is 30%. But you can choose to be taxed on *half your gain* at your top tax rate. However, under this option, gains over £5,000 are then taxed at the full income rate.

Chapter 13

Unit Trusts

Jumping in at the shallow end

If you have read Chapter 12, on investment, you may have decided to invest some of your money in shares. But you may still have some reservations about it. Do any of the following descriptions apply to you?

● You would like to invest in shares, but really know next to nothing about the Stock Exchange.
● You are prepared to take some risk, but you are keen to minimise it as much as possible.
● After providing for your essential savings, life insurance and so on, you have only a small amount available for a venture on to the stock market.
● You have little spare time and cannot afford to devote it to studying the stock market or dealing with the administrative chores that shareholding involves.

If any of these descriptions fit, you may find that investing through a unit trust is the answer for you.

What a unit trust is

A unit trust is a mechanism to enable a large number of investors to pool their money in a single fund and put it under professional investment management.

The important thing about a unit trust is that it *is* a trust. That means it is subject to strict rules, and has to have a trustee or watchdog, to make sure the rules are kept. The management company has to account to the trustee for every last penny in the unit trust fund.

This means that unit trusts can safely grow very big indeed, with many thousands of investors investing between them many millions of pounds.

There are currently around 230 different trusts operating in Britain. They are set up and organized by management companies which advertise for investors to join the trust and arrange for the money to be invested. For these services the investors pay them a fee.

The advantages

● Spreading your risk.
● Expert management of your investments.
● Simplicity in buying.

Spreading your risk

In the same way it is difficult and expensive to divide a small investment into a number of different shareholdings. Stockbrokers will not like it or help you to do it, and the cost for each transaction will be high. Thus the small investor runs a risk of "putting too many eggs into one basket."

A unit trust fund will always be invested in at least 20 shares – that is one of the rules, so every investor has a stake in all the holdings, however small his own investment may be.

This does not mean that you cannot lose money in a unit trust. But it does mean that you are unlikely to do much worse than the average of the whole stock market, and you will not lose all your money overnight because the one company in which you happen to have invested goes broke.

Expert management of your investments

If every investor in a unit trust had his own portfolio of shares and tried to hire a professional adviser to look after it, the cost would be astronomical and there wouldn't be enough advisers to go round.

By investing jointly in a single portfolio of shares, unit trust investors can share the costs of advice between them in an economical way. The advice unit trusts get inevitably varies in quality, but the same would be true if each investor had his own personal adviser.

To make a success of investing you need to hold quite a large number of shares and be prepared to move your money around quite actively in response to circumstances. But the more shares you hold and the more you buy and sell, the more administrative chores there are.

In a unit trust the drudgery is taken care of by the management company. You just sit back and let them get on with it.

WISEGUIDE

Successful investment takes time and expertise. If you lack either of these you should consider a unit trust.

Simplicity in buying & selling

For the really small investor, unit trusts are really the only feasible way of buying shares. Stockbrokers are not anxious to take on uneconomical small amounts, and, even if they do, their charges take up too much of the total capital. Unit trusts will often accept as little as £50 or less.

We are going to describe unit trusts in detail; it may seem to be a complicated procedure to buy them, but all you have to do is to look up the price of a trust in a newspaper, work out the total cost of the number you want to buy, fill in your cheque or money order and send it to the managers. You can make a "once-and-for-all" purchase, or join a monthly savings scheme. Selling is just as simple.

WISEGUIDE

If you have less than £1,000 to invest it is not really sensible to "go it alone" on the stock market. And unit trusts are good for those with a lot more capital.

The disadvantages

The theory of unit trust investment is a sensible one, but there are some inevitable snags.

● It is less exciting than investing on your own

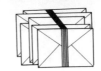

• You miss out on the chance of making a "killing" by putting all your money into one share which "goes through the roof"

• Not all unit trusts are equally successful. You could (very rarely) be unlucky and hit on one whose advisers are even less successful than you would be alone.

Before going any further it is vital to get one thing clear:

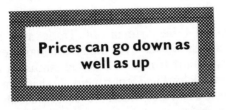

Prices can go down as well as up

Investing in a unit trust does not remove the risk of investing in shares. It just reduces it. If you are not prepared to or cannot risk your money, do not put it into shares even through a unit trust.

How unitholders are protected

A formidable battery of defences protect unitholders.

The law

The law governing unit trust operations is laid down in The Prevention of Fraud (Investments) Act. Its important stipulations are:
1) The unit trust management company must have a reasonable amount of capital behind it
2) It must have a trustee which is also a substantial concern and must not have any ties of interest with the management company. It has the job of safeguarding the unitholders' interests
3) It must operate strictly according to the rules, set out in its trust deed
4) Unless the management company obeys the rules, the trust will not be authorised
5) Only authorised unit trusts may advertise for investors
6) No unit trust may indulge in door-to-door selling.

The trust deed

Every detail of the trusts method of operation are laid out in its trust deed. The trust deeds differ between one unit trust and another on minor matters but the main guide lines are all the same. These guide lines are laid down by the Department of Trade and Industry which has the job of interpreting the unit trust law.

In particular the trust deed lays out:
1. How the unit prices are calculated
2. What the managers can charge
3. Some general investment principles
   a) The managers must not invest more than 5% of the fund

in any one share (in some recent trust deeds this has risen to 7%).

b) The fund must not own more than 10% of any company.

c) The fund must be invested only in securities registered on a recognised stock exchange. (Some trust deeds do allow a small amount to be invested in unquoted shares, but a unit trust may *never* put money into other types of investment, such as property or antiques.)

The Department of Trade & Industry

The Government's Department of Trade and Industry has practically limitless power over unit trust managers because it can take away a unit trust's authorised status. All trust deeds have to be agreed by the Department, and it can at any time decide to impose new rules which the trusts must abide by.

The trustee

The trustee is usually a bank (and sometimes an insurance company). Its most important job is to hold the shares of the fund on the unitholder's behalf. So no-one can get up to anything with the fund's investments without the trustee knowing about it.

The trustee also has an overall responsibility to ensure the rules of the trust are being kept.

The Association of Unit Trust Managers

About two thirds of all unit trusts belong to the association and its standards influence all of them. In particular the association vets advertisements to prevent misleading claims.

What it costs

When you buy unit trusts there are certain costs involved. Unitholders must pay:

- The management company for its administrative and advisory services (plus a profit to make it worth the company's while)

- The normal cost of investment (see chapter 12)

- A unit trust instrument duty of $\frac{1}{4}$%.

These have to be taken into account when the price of the units are calculated. There are, in fact, two prices applying to a unit at any time:

The Offer Price – the price at which the unit can be bought.
The Bid Price – the price at which it can be sold back to the management.

Strict rules apply to the exact way these prices are arrived at. For any given value of the fund there is a maximum the offer price can be, and a minimum the bid price can be. In practice no unit will have a maximum offer price *and* a minimum bid price at the same time. The gap between the two would be unnecessarily large and competition between unit trusts means they work on a smaller margin.

Generally the gap between the offer price and the bid price is about 5–6%. If the offer price is 50p, then the bid price is around 47p.

Usually the offer price is at its permitted maximum and the

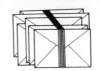

bid price is something above the lowest level allowed. Sometimes, however, the bid price is at its permitted minimum and and the offer price is consequently lower than it could be.

The maximum offer price=the unit share of the fund+the manager's *initial Service Charge*+a sum based on the cost of buying the fund's investments+the unit trust duty+an amount of up to 1% to "round off" the price to a workable amount.

The minimum bid price=the unit share of the fund−a sum based on the cost of selling the fund's investments − an amount of up to 1% to "round off" the price to a workable amount.

The most important part of these costs is the manager's charges: **Management charges**

1. *The Initial Service Charge*
   This is the charge mentioned above. It is expressed as a percentage of the offer price of the unit, and paid when the unit is bought.

2. *The Management Fee*
   This is paid every six months when the requisite amount is taken out of the fund's income. It is expressed as a percentage of the price of the unit at the time.

The amount the managers can charge is limited by more rules:

1. The initial service charge must not be more than 5%.
2. The initial service charge and the management fee together must not add up to more than $13\frac{1}{4}\%$ over 20 years.
3. This is not a rule, but in practice the management fee is not allowed to be more than $\frac{1}{2}\%$ a year.

Unit trust managers normally follow one of these two formulas: **Normal charges**

1. An *initial charge* of 5% (5p in the £) and a *management fee* of $\frac{3}{8}\%$ (37·5p for every £100 invested in the fund).
2. An *initial charge* of $3\frac{1}{4}\%$ (3·75p in the £) and a *management fee* of $\frac{1}{2}\%$ (50p for every £100 invested in the fund).

Both these combinations work out at the permitted maximum. Some unit trusts charge less. Usually these only allow the investment of large amounts (£500 or more).

WISEGUIDE

A unit trust investment should be regarded as a long term venture. If you buy and sell too quickly you may not cover your costs.

Choosing a unit trust

There are now some 250 different unit trusts operating in Britain.

A common mistake is to think they are all pretty much the same. In fact there are some important differences.

a) The quality of investment management.
b) The size; a unit trust fund can be around £100 million or less than £1 million.
c) Their objectives – particularly as far as income is concerned.
d) The minimum amount you may invest.
e) Their charges.
f) Other services linked to the units.

The differences

You will find lists of unit trusts and their prices on the financial pages of most newspapers and financial magazines. Several newspapers also carry regular articles on unit trusts in their columns which deal with money matters.

The Association of Unit Trust Managers will supply you with details about all its members, but it will not of course, recommend one rather than another. The Association publishes an annual directory. The address is: 306 Salisbury House, Finsbury Circus, London E.C.2.

You can get advice from your bank manager or stockbroker or any other professional advisers. It will not cost you anything – the management company pays the commission to the stockbroker or bank.

You may come to your own conclusions about the trust's investment management by looking at the shares it is actually invested in. The managers must publish a list every six months, and will gladly send enquirers the latest one.

WISEGUIDE

Unit trusts *do* vary. It pays to be selective.

The managers

Well over sixty companies manage unit trusts. Some of them operate only one trust while others run a whole range of them.

There are:

1. Unit trust management companies who concentrate entirely on this business.
2. Banks and insurance companies who have unit trust departments.

By far the most important distinction between management is the QUALITY of their investment advisers.

Some unit trust managements employ their own advisers. Others employ the services of an outside concern. The trusts which are part of a larger investment group will normally share the common facilities.

It is worthwhile to take some trouble to find out what sort of facilities a trust has to draw on. A trust whose investments are managed in a large department backed by researchers, analysts and mechanical aids, should, in theory, do better than one which has to share the attention of one or two harassed advisers with

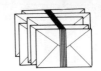

a large number of other trusts.

But, and it is a big but, in the last resort, investment is a skill. You can find investment advisers doing very successfully in unpropitious circumstances and others who, with all the mechanical aids in the world, are not going to be very good at their job. Indeed, it often turns out that some trusts in a group are a lot better than others.

At this point to try to assess future prospects you must fall back on a study of past performance.

Studying performance

Most newspapers and financial magazines publish figures which indicate how unit trusts have performed at their job of earning income and achieving capital growth for the unitholders. There can be scarcely any other business whose progress is charted so thoroughly.

In studying the charts and tables, keep the following in mind:

- *Short term comparisons do not indicate much.* Any number of incidental factors can affect them. Three years is a reasonable period over which to judge whether a unit is a consistently good performer. Many unit trusts have not been in existence that long, however. You may not want to miss them. It all depends on how cautious you are.

- Some performance tables measure only capital growth (the rise in the price of the units), which ignores the fact that some trusts pay out more income than others.

WISEGUIDE

The past can never be a complete guide to the future. The factors which have made unit trust successful in the past may be disappearing while you are studying the figures.

Investment objectives

Some trusts have the achievement of high income as their primary objective, while others are prepared to sacrifice income to achieve the maximum capital growth. There are a number of reasons why the two do not normally go together.

Yields on unit trusts vary with conditions in the stock market. At the time of writing yields are quite high and the average unit trust is yielding 3–4%. An income "specialist" should yield more than this. Some trusts pursue a policy aimed at achieving 8% or more..

An "all-out" capital growth fund will usually yield 2% or less. A number of these reinvest any income automatically on the unitholder's behalf. This should help their performance.

Quite a number of trusts aim for a "middle of the road" policy aiming for average income and reasonable growth.

WISEGUIDE

Your unit trust cannot escape stock market trends entirely, but you should do better in a trust managed by experts, than if you invest yourself.

Specialist Trusts

A number of trusts restrict their investment to a particular class of shares. These specialists include:

I *Investment Trusts*, that is companies whose business is in investing in shares in the similar way as a unit trust. A unit trust invested in investment trust shares obviously has a simply enormous spread of investments, and multiple investment expertise.

II *The Financial Sector*. A number of trusts specialise in shares in banks, insurance companies and the like, including some investment trusts. This policy is held to give particularly good chances of capital appreciation in some circumstances. Several such specialists have in fact done particularly well over the years.

III *Commodities*. These trusts invest not in commodities themselves, of course, which is against the rules, but in companies in the commodities business. The point of this is the very high yield to be achieved from such a policy.

IV *Investment Overseas*. A number of trusts invest exclusively in the United States. One concentrates on Australia and two trusts now invest entirely in the interesting Japan market.

There was a time when a trust which invested overseas at all was classed as a specialist, but more and more unit trusts are now taking a few foreign shares in their portfolios.

WISEGUIDE

Specialist trusts are mainly for people who invest in a number of trusts and want to concentrate their investments in particular areas.

How much can you invest?

● The majority of unit trusts will accept investments of £100 or less and quite a number will accept as little as £50.

● There are a few trusts which will accept even less than £50.

● Increasingly, though, trusts are requiring a minimum investment of more than £100. This does not mean that the smaller investor is being eased out – the various savings schemes, and savings plans linked to assurance, are discussed in chapter 8.

There is a group of trusts which will only accept investments of really substantial amounts—£1,000 or more. These trusts will generally charge less than the normal because larger investments are more economical to handle.

Other services

● *Savings Plans*. Some trusts run schemes whereby you may invest small amounts – such as £5 or £10 – in the trust on a regular monthly basis. These have now been outdated by the more rewarding unit trust linked insurance plans.

● *Children's Gift Plans.* Quite a number of trusts have a mechanism which allows you to invest money on behalf of a child.

● *Share Exchange Schemes.* You may sometimes be allowed to exchange shares you already hold for units in a unit trust.

Unless you particularly need them, other services should not be allowed to weigh against basic considerations.

WISEGUIDE

● Having made your choice of trust you may write or telephone to the management company and they will tell you how to apply for units. Normally you will buy units at the price reigning on the date your cheque is received.

   The manager will return any money which is above the cost of an exact number of units.

● Alternatively, you can make the arrangements through your bank, or other advisers.

● You will then receive a certificate telling you how many units you own in the fund. Hold on to this as you must return it when you want to sell.

● You can then study the progress of your units from the prices quoted every day in the financial pages of most of the national daily newspapers.

● The next you will hear from your management company will probably be when they make a half yearly distribution of the fund's income. At this time you will get a cheque for your unit's share of the fund's income plus a certificate telling you how much tax has been paid. Hold on to this carefully, too, for reasons explained below.

● At the same time you will probably receive your trust's half-yearly report. This will show the investments the fund holds, and accounts.

● If you want to buy more units, the management will be only too pleased. You will be able to add to your holding in quite small amounts.

● If you want to sell your units, you write to the management company enclosing your certificates. You will receive payment within a few days.

● Unit trusts, like ordinary investors, receive dividends on their investments after income tax has been paid. The certificate you receive with your distribution will show how much income tax has been paid for each unit.

● If you are not liable for income tax you can claim the tax paid

Becoming a unit holder:

Income tax

back from the Inland Revenue. If you pay surtax you must make up the difference. (At present the whole question of surtax is under review.)

Capital gains tax When you sell, you may if you have a profit have to pay capital gains tax, as with any other investment. But if the total amount realised on all sales of investments is less than £500 in any one year, no gains tax is payable.

If your sale comes to more than £500 there is an important relief available to you. A unit trust itself pays capital gains tax on the profits that it makes on the sales of shares in the trust's portfolio, so to that extent you don't have to pay the tax all over again. This relief works by the unit trust telling you, when it pays your income distribution, what the gains on which it has paid tax amount to.

All you have to do is to keep these tax certificates and hand them over to the tax inspector when you declare your gain after a sale. He will calculate the relief due to you.

Is it for me? Unit trusts were devised to make the business of investment simpler and to some extent safer. There is no doubt that they succeed at this, although some are better at it than others.

On the other hand, unit trust investment lacks some of the glamour there is in making your own decisions on the stock market.

For the smaller investor, unit trusts provide the only effective way of investing in shares at all.

WISEGUIDE

If you have already decided to put some money into shares, unit trusts provide a sensible way of doing so. The simple golden rule is to decide which managers you can trust; write to them for advice on which is the best one to suit you.

Non-monetary Investments

Many people who would not dream of "having a flutter" on the Stock Market will quite happily walk into an antique shop and spend tens or hundreds of £'s on a piece of furniture or a painting. Since the end of the 1939–45 war ordinary people have had increasing sums of money to spare – and many have started putting this money into fine art (antiques, paintings), diamonds, wine and other non-monetary investments.

World record prices for various sales are regularly reported in the newspapers: £2·3 million for the Velazquez *Portrait of Juan de Pareja* (record auction price, November 1970); £78,000 for the Charles I inkstand (record for a single piece of silver, July 1970); and £94,500 for the Kuan-Yao, Sung dynasty bottle (record for a work of art other than a painting, October 1970).

A plethora of books, periodicals, and specialised articles on investment in non-monetary objects describe the market and themselves help to boost sales.

How it works

There are three rules that most experts give to people about to invest in fine art. These are: go for quality, rarity, and something that you like.

Points to notice

● Quality always commands a premium price over the run-of-the-mill items in the same category. An item which is rare, particularly if it is useful, also fetches a good price. And if you cannot afford to pay heed to the first two rules buy something you like. It may have a quality which will appeal to someone else some day.

● Know the approximate value of what you are buying. This way you can roughly estimate your potential profit when you sell. An antique will not make you a beefy profit just because it is an antique. So, if you know the item which you have bought is not in first class condition, or doesn't work properly, you must limit your profit estimate for it – then you won't be disappointed when you sell.

● Find out all you can about the particular object or field of fine art you intend to invest in. There are many museums, art galleries and houses with collections of historic interest open to the public. Dealers and auctioneers rely heavily on these places for their information. Use them fully. Salerooms are open several days in advance of auctions so that potential buyers can inspect the stock. Experts here will give impartial advice about lots coming up for sale: although they stress that this advice is "without responsibility", it is opinion. At auctions, most people go away without buying. They sit and learn. The big London salerooms start their sales at about 11 am and 2.30 pm during their season, October to July.

● Try to buy from a reputable seller; and always get a receipt for insurance purposes. You may buy from:

(1) *Antique shops.* But remember that their mark-up can be up to 100% on what they paid for the item. However, the quality of the goods may be excellent because dealers often renovate before selling.

(2) *London salerooms.* The most famous are Sotheby's in Bond Street; Christie's in King Street, St. James's; Phillips Son & Neale in Blenheim Street, New Bond Street; Knight Frank & Rutley, 20 Hanover Square, W1; and W. and F. C. Bonham in Montpelier Street, SW7. These and others advertise forthcoming sales every Tuesday in *The Times* and *The Daily Telegraph*; and in other newspapers and periodicals.

(3) *Provincial salerooms and country house sales.* These have been attracting increasing numbers of dealers, tourists, and individual buyers outside their immediate locality and prices have become inflated in recent years.

(4) *Regular antique fairs.* The best-known are the (expensive) Grosvenor House Fair held every June in the Grosvenor House Hotel: the Antique Dealers' Fair has a year-round kiosk in the hotel; and the twice-yearly Chelsea Antiques Fair, in March and September. There is normally an admission charge. All items up for sale are vetted by a committee of experts for authenticity. The Chelsea Fair is held in the Town Hall, King's Road.

(5) *Permanent Antique Marts.* Prices in these are frequently inflated.

WISEGUIDE

Prices in these fields can vary enormously depending on where you buy.

Is it for me? Should I invest in fine art?

For   ● The value of antiques, paintings, oriental carpets, and other collectors' items is continually going up. The table, taken from *The Times*-Sotheby Index, shows the type of increase in value registered in specific categories over the last 10 and 20 years. The Index is only an approximate guide to price changes, and is compiled from items illustrated in saleroom catalogues, but not from items of exceptional value which would distort the figures. However, the figures are influenced by the appearance of large and

How prices have multiplied

How prices have multiplied*

Type of investment	Price increase: 1951-70 – 1960-70		Comments
English silver	5½	2½	1968 was a boom year. By 1970 prices were back to their 1966 levels.
Impressionist pictures	15½	3	1970 failed to produce the spectacular prices paid for Impressionists' work in general the year before. Prices actually fell 8% below the average 1969 levels. But Monet's work raised very good prices.
Old Master prints	31	10	
Drawings	20	6	Quality (rather than decorative value) commanded highest prices, which rose in some cases by tens of £1,000's.
Modern painting	20½	3	
Oriental porcelain	22	5	Prices did not have such a good year as in 1969 because, following the good records reached in the previous year, too many people brought T'ang pottery and Sung dynasty wares to the salerooms. The early Ming blue and white wares, more rarely seen at auction, achieved good prices; best pieces continued to command a premium.
English pictures	9½	3½	Watercolours are currently fashionable. Victorian and marine pictures continue to fetch good prices.
Old Master pictures	(1951-69) 7	(1960-69) 3	
English glass	(1951-69) 8½	(1960-69) 4	Prices likely to increase steadily. Tremendous collectors' interest at all price levels.

Average price increases over 10- and 20-year periods, from The Times-Sotheby Index surveys.

good collections in the auction rooms which have not been put up for sale for a time.

It shows that in 10 years (1960–70) the price of Old Master prints has gone up ten times (1,000%); oriental porcelain, five times; English watercolours, three times; and Impressionist pictures, three times. Retail prices in general went up from a base of 100 in 1962 to only 147·8 in 1971: by less than half in a similar period.

157

● Small sums of money can be invested. Seven in every 10 items sold at Sotheby's and at Christie's fetch less than £100, and two in every 10 at Sotheby's fetch £20 or less. Books, records, small icons, stamps are among the least expensive buys.

● You can enjoy many investments while they are making you money: things like paintings, carpets, glass and furniture. The furniture may also be a substitute for a piece you need but which, if modern, would not make you money but decrease in value with the years.

Against   ● Before you start counting real profits, remember to offset any of the following "losses" you may have incurred:

(a) *Inflation.* In 1970 the rise in retail prices was 8% over the year before. If this is the average rate of inflation you must aim to keep up with it by the time you sell. Changes in the kind of antiques or paintings which are "fashionable" may prevent this.

(b) *The Cost of Insurance.* Premiums vary so much that it would be misleading to specify an average rate. Factors considered are: locality (suburbs and country tend to attract lower rates than town centres); internal and police protection; your personal insurance record. Items are insured for cost price, not replacement value – unless you ask for this, or for a yearly rate of appreciation to be written into your policy. Also remember that a large, bulky, difficult-to-steal piece of furniture is less likely to be stolen (and will cost less to insure) than a small piece of silver or jewellery. Many insurance companies will not underwrite unmounted diamonds; you may have to go to Lloyds. If possible, keep a receipt, a photograph of the item, and a valuation for expensive pieces.

(c) *Valuation Costs:* are free if you take an item to the counter at Sotheby's or Christie's. But a valuation for insurance, or probate, costs a minimum of £10 in London or £15 in the country. It falls from 1% on items worth up to £10,000 to $\frac{1}{4}$% on those over £100,000. A local dealer may be less expensive.

(d) *Capital Gains Tax:* payable where proceeds for each item exceed £1,000. You pay no tax on sales below this amount.

(e) *Dealer's or saleroom's percentage* on items they sell for you. This varies from about 10% on jewellery, wine and objects of vertu to 15% on the sale price of paintings, drawings and Japanese works of art. The personal column of a newspaper may be a less expensive way to sell.

● Antiques are a form of investment which have no market value – apart from that which a buyer is prepared to pay. The growth rate is therefore irregular and varies according to when you sell (except on quality items). The same painting which sells for £500 one day at auction may raise £1,000 if sold on a better day. The only way to ensure a minimum return is to place a reserve price on the item: if the price is not realised the item is bought in for you and you lose the auctioneer's fee.

● Clearly, you can lose as much from dabbling in the fine art market as you can in any other form of speculation. Do not buy if prices are too high: as silver was in 1968. If prices fall, you will have to keep the item several years until they rise sufficiently again. In 1970 silverware prices were on average down to almost half their 1968 levels.

Fluctuations

When Stock Market prices fall and there is less money about so do antique prices in general – but not prices that are paid for items of exceptional quality. The rush into non-monetary investments in 1968–69 in the wake of devaluation was a response to a currency crisis not to the Stock Market low. Understandably, perhaps, there was a rush into antique silverware. This was ridiculous from the investment point of view for the relationship between the price of silver and the value of antique silver-ware is more psychological than real.

WISEGUIDE

Antiques are not a short-term investment – unless you think you have the knowledge and the money to speculate. They are a safer long-term investment.

Note

But, although many would deny it, there are definite fashions in the fine art market. In 1970–71 watercolours have been popular for investment purposes. When a book is published on, say, icons, icons increase in value.

Fashions

The decision by Sotheby's to open a new saleroom in Belgravia exclusively for the sale of Victoriana and 19th-century items should marginally push up the value of these. Victoriana has, in fact, been selling well for some time. It is part of a move into less expensive antiques and fine art now that traditional markets have passed out of the buying power of all but the richest investors and museums. Hence also the popularity of prints and etchings rather than paintings.

Diamonds—How it works

A diamond's value is determined by the four C's: carat, cut, colour and clarity. The best investment is a stone of at least two carats, finely cut so that it sparkles like mad, and a clean blue or white colour with few scratches. Over the last 10 years this type of stone has doubled or trebled in value.

Is it for me? Should I invest in diamonds?

The bigger diamonds are becoming increasingly rare and are in great demand, not only in London but as far afield as Japan, now a big market. These are a good investment.

For

● Unmounted stones are free of the 55% purchase tax levied on mounted stones. These are best, apart from really fine antique diamond jewellery, for investment purposes.

Against Diamonds are not for the small investor. The smallest diamond you should buy for investment purposes is one weighing one carat or more. This will cost you a cool £850 (compared with £300 10 years ago).

● There are various diamond investment schemes aimed at the small investor. Many are infinitely more advantageous to the seller than to the customer. They normally comprise a small, sealed package of two stones, sometimes with a certificate stating the weight of the stones in the package. Unless the seller is prepared to state in writing that he will buy the pack back from you AT A SPECIFIED PRICE, OR RATE OF INCREASED VALUE PER YEAR – it is unwise to invest. If you sell back to a merchant, he will give you the market value – minus his percentage. To make a profit, this would mean keeping the stones some years.

● In 1970 sales of diamonds were 23% lower than the previous year. There is at present a glut of small diamonds on the market. (These are the types normally mounted in engagement rings.)

WISEGUIDE Remember you have to find a buyer in order to sell.

**Wine—
How it works** Some salerooms hold regular wine auctions: the minimum quantity that can be bought is normally two cases = 24 bottles. Wines are normally sold FOB (free on board ship i.e. before tax). So for each case add £6·90 to vintage port; £4·70 to claret; and about £5 to wine to cover the costs of duty, freight, final delivery, agency fee, and insurance. Sale catalogues specify exact amounts. Wine and spirits may be taken away or you can arrange bond (storage) for about 25p to 50p per case per year.

● Do your homework. Find out all you can beforehand about the wine you want to buy. Go to the tasting session the day before the sale.

Is it for me? Should I invest in wine?

For You can buy wines and spirits at auction at lower prices than you would have to pay for the same at your local off-licence. If you cannot afford to buy by the case-load alone: form a syndicate of friends and buy collectively.

● You can leave a commission with the auctioneer to buy a lot of wines for you if you cannot attend the sale in person. There is normally no charge for this service.

● Investment-wise, claret and vintage port are best value-for-money. These are what dealers buy in bulk. Much may be learned by watching dealers and bids.

Wine

Sold at £3 per case

The lot consisted of 3 cases of twelve bottles
each of 1970 vintage Rheingau,
Johannisberger Erntebringer.

Sold at £10 per case

The lot consisted of 2 cases of
24 half-bottles each of
1955 vintage claret, Château Tronquoy-Lalande,
cru bourgeois supérieur, Saint-Estèphe.

Sold at £18 per dozen

The lot consisted of 3 dozen bottles
of French bottled Burgundy,
Charmes-Chambertin, 1959 vintage.
This was one of several lots offered
duty-paid but available in bond.

Sold at £4·75 per case

The lot consisted of 3 cases
of 12 bottles each of a full-bodied
red wine from the Madiran district,
Pyrénées-Atlantiques, vintage 1968 Château de Peyros,
appellation Madiran controlée.

**Examples of prices of selected wines
from an auction at Christie's April 1st, 1971.**

Ports and clarets are not short-term investments. Claret increases in value gradually: but you need to keep a good new vintage ten years before re-selling. Port values jump after about five years; a good vintage should be kept at least 15 years after it was made.

● While savings can be made in the per bottle price of wines and spirits bought at auction – this does not necessarily follow. Bidding tends to start at a level near that of the normal retail price. Therefore if second, third or more bids are made you could find yourself paying more than the retail price, particularly on wines, if you go on bidding.

● Avoid what are called "end of bin" sales: they are just that.

Always go to an auction knowing exactly what you are prepared to pay. Never go above this limit in the bidding.

Against

**Bids per dozen
and prices per bottle**

Per dozen	Per bottle
£7·50	£0·63
£18·00	£1·50
£9·50	£0·79
£20·00	£1·67
£12·50	£1·04
£50·00	£4·17

Chapter 15

Making a Will

Everyone should make a will. Too many people do not think about this rather morbid subject until old age makes it even more difficult to think about – or an accident or unexpected death makes it too late. It is far more sensible to face the subject first when you are young – when death is a remote event. Once you have thought about it, it becomes easier to reconsider as life goes on and your wishes change.

Why make a will? Dying intestate (that means without making a will) is inefficient and irresponsible even if you have only a little money or property to leave. Even where the rules for the distribution of the property of those who do not make wills are the same as a person would have wished if he or she had made a will, there are still excellent reasons for making one.

For ● The process of making a will, especially if you take professional advice, provides an opportunity – in fact it puts pressure on you – to consider your affairs, not just from the point of view of provision for your dependants and estate duty (that is a tax which may have to be paid on what you leave behind), but also from the viewpoint of all other taxation and provision for your own lifetime.

● A will allows you to select those who will administer your estate as Executors. These are the people who will see that your wishes are carried out. It may be that you will choose, say, your nearest relatives, who would look after things if you did not make a will, but it is often better if their work is shared with someone else.

● A will gives you the chance to give the executors wider powers of investment of your money than they would have under the law. This can mean a better financial future for your family.

● A will can set out a financial plan which carefully considers your own family's particular circumstances. This personal element is lacking if you do not make a will.

● Looking after an estate, if there is a will, is generally just a little cheaper and easier than if there isn't one.

Against Nothing.

WISEGUIDE

Whatever your circumstances or age, making a will is a good idea.

How to make a will

If you begrudge solicitors their quite low charges for drawing up a will, you are of course free to make it yourself. Before doing so, however, you would be wise to think again. The rules of will making are many and technical; compliance with them is all essential. The phrasing of the document is also important; what to you means one thing may, in law, mean something totally different. The advantage of consulting a solicitor is that he will not only make sure that the will he prepares for you is correct as to form and content, but he will also draw your attention to matters of which you may not have thought, or of which you may not have been aware.

If at all possible, use a solicitor in drawing up your will.

If, after reflection, you decide that your wishes are simple, your affairs straightforward and that you still want to do it yourself, buy a book that tells you how to set about it. Do not be tempted by forms that you can buy in stationers: these are sometimes misleading and you may be diverted from expressing yourself as you wish to, if you follow their particular formulae. Stick firmly to the rules the book explains and, if you have the slightest doubt about what you are doing, stop and think again. A badly made will is often worse than no will, and remember you must have two people who cannot be beneficiaries under your will, to witness it. They need not read it.

Choice of executors

Being an executor is no mere honorary office; it carries responsibility and may involve a good deal of work. Executors should, therefore, be chosen with care.

● The first and obvious choice is your husband or wife – he or she is likely to be the principal beneficiary and, having much at stake, should have some say in the administration of the estate. He or she may, however, be fairly elderly by the time the executorship begins, so the appointment of a co-executor is advisable. A child who has attained majority might be a suitable choice.

● Another possibility is a family friend who has some knowledge or experience of managing business affairs, or a professional adviser, a lawyer or accountant. A frequent choice is that of the solicitor who has drawn the will. Here, what is known as a "charging clause" will have to be included in the will as solicitors do not normally do this sort of work for nothing. This is usually no real additional burden on your estate, as executors generally prove wills with the assistance of solicitors and fees for that service come out of the estate too.

● So far the choice has been between individuals, but the field is wider. The larger banks all have Executor and Trustee Departments who will take on the job, again for a fee. Details of the services provided can be found in the explanatory booklets published by these banks. A bank may be a sensible choice when no obvious individual presents him or herself for appointment, or when it is possible that family frictions will require an executor who is completely uninvolved. Additionally, a bank will have wide-ranging experience in financial matters and, unlike humans, does not die. If continuing trusts are involved the bank would not need to be replaced as a trustee; the death of individual trustees makes necessary appointment of new ones.

● The Public Trustee and Trust Corporations are possible but less frequent choices. The advantages here are much the same as with banks. All these institutional executors like to see the will in draft before it is executed and have their own particular forms of wording for their appointment.

Courtesy demands that all executors should be consulted before being named. Although an executor cannot be compelled to act as such (even if he has agreed to being named), there is often a feeling of moral obligation which forces him to take on the job even though he would have refused had he been consulted.

Finally, apart from all the business aspects of the administration of the estate, an executor has to arrange the funeral. The right approach to this and to other matters involving personal contact with the bereaved relatives is important; it is more likely that an individual relative or friend can supply this, rather than professional advisers or members of the staff of an institution, however pleasant they may be.

WISEGUIDE

Choose an executor in whom you have absolute trust and confidence.

When your will may be upset

A perfectly valid will can be challenged. Before 1939, in England and Wales at least, a man could without just cause cut off his family with the proverbial shilling and leave his all to a mistress or a home for horses. But with the passing of the Inheritance (Family Provision) Act, 1938, certain members of the family may apply to the executors and the Court for reasonable provision to be made for them out of the estate. A surviving husband or wife, a son under 21, an unmarried daughter, and any child who is incapable of maintaining him or herself because of mental or physical disability, are the dependent relatives who today are protected from unfair discrimination.

Other challenges to wills depend on proof that they are invalid, for example, because they fail to comply with the formal

requirements of a will, because they are forged or because the testator, at the time of executing the will was of unsound mind.

Once made your will endures until it is revoked. If made in early life it may become inappropriate. The best way to remedy such a situation is to make a new will and express it to revoke all previous wills.

WISEGUIDE

Make sure that your will expresses your intentions. You should remember that marriage revokes a will, unless it was made in contemplation of that marriage.

If you live in Scotland, check the position because the law there is in many respects different from England and Wales.

Estate duty

Estate duty is no more and no less than one of the means used by the government to raise revenue. To some extent, however, it is still a voluntary tax, although opportunities for opting out are narrowing. It is a specialist's subject, but is worth some general description, if only to show why and when the specialist should be consulted.

When it is levied

Basically estate duty is levied on all property which "passes" on a death and, so as to spread the net wider, certain property is "deemed" to pass on death. Some of the main categories of dutiable property are:

● Property of which the deceased was competent to dispose on his death. This definition makes dutiable all the estate that passes under the will or intestacy.

● The capital representing any share in a settlement which the deceased enjoyed by way of a life interest or under a discretionary trust.

● Property with which the deceased had parted in the last seven years of his life and property whenever given away in which he retained some form of interest.

● Partnership assets passing to surviving partners without their having to provide any consideration in return.

Rates of duty

If an estate is liable to estate duty, it will be divided into slices and varying rates of duty will apply to each slice. The duty rates are then averaged to give an "estate rate".

Exemptions from estate duty

In order to calculate the total value of an estate and so discover whether duty is payable and, if so, how much, certain items of property may be exempt. The most important of these are:

● The first £12,500.

● Property comprised within a "surviving spouse" exemption, i.e. property in which the deceased had a life interest under the terms of the will of his or her previously deceased spouse.

Example

The total duty on an estate of £45,000 will be:—

£12,500 — £17,500 = £1,250
£17,500 — £30,000 = £3,750
£30,000 — £40,000 = £4,500
£40,000 — £45,000 = £3,000
—————
£12,500

Estate Rate = $\dfrac{£12,500}{£45,000} \times 100$

= 27·7%

Value of Estate		Rate on slice	Maximum sum payable on slice
Exceeding	*But not above*		
£12,500	£17,500	25%	£1,250
£17,500	£30,000	30%	£3,750
£30,000	£40,000	45%	£4,500
£40,000	£80,000	60%	£24,000
£80,000	£150,000	65%	£45,000
£150,000	£300,000	70%	£105,000
£300,000	£500,000	75%	£150,000
£500,000	£750,000	80%	£200,000
£750,000		85%	

● Gifts and settlements made in consideration of marriage by certain specified relatives of the bride and bridegroom, or by either of them to each other. These cannot exceed £5,000 in the case of any one donor for any one marriage when the donor is a parent or grandparent or party to the marriage; in the case of donors who are aunts, uncles, brothers and sisters or others the limit is £1,000.

● Gifts forming part of the normal expenditure of the deceased, e.g. under 7-year covenants.

● Gifts not exceeding £500 in the case of each donee, even though made within the last 7 years of the deceased donor's life.

WISEGUIDE

Check which parts of your estate will be exempt from estate duty.

How to reduce the estate duty bill

The first rule of estate duty saving is that not nearly so much saving can be effected by your will as by taking action in your lifetime. After all, the will operates only on death and by then the estate duty hammer has fallen.

Planning in one's lifetime takes the form of reducing one's estate and otherwise utilising the exemptions as far as possible. Clearly the scope for saving increases with the size of original estate but savings may be made even in small estates and the benefit gained may be relatively as or more valuable to those who inherit.

The mitigation of estate duty is of greatest importance to you if it is likely that your dependants, such as your spouse, children or other relatives, will survive your death. If you have none of these you may not consider it worthwhile to reduce the liability; but if you do not wish your hard won savings to be snatched away overnight it is well worth paying for some good advice.

WISEGUIDE

The best way to save duty on your estate is to think about it long before you expect to die. Take expert advice as soon as possible.

UK Taxes & You

Each year as winter gives way to spring we have to face one, usually chilling, experience, the annual budget. This is the time when the Chancellor of the Exchequer fixes for the year the amount of tax we will have to pay. This chapter will take you through all the details in the British tax system. Where necessary you must refer back to earlier chapters which mention taxation as it applies to particular aspects of saving and spending.
Taxation in this country is broadly divided into two main classes:

The taxes we pay

These include all the taxes which we pay but do not notice because they are hidden. They include purchase tax, excise and customs duties, selective employment tax and stamp duties. Indirect taxes account for approximately one-third of the total taxation collected each year. You pay them automatically if you buy or use the items upon which they are imposed.

Indirect taxes

These are the taxes which we will discuss in this book as far as they relate to individuals.

Direct taxes

We are not concerned here with the taxation of companies and similar bodies of persons.

The taxes relating to individuals are three main ones that affect most of us most of the time. They are:

- Income tax
- Surtax
- Capital gains tax.

Another form of direct taxation is Estate Duty, which is a tax paid on the value of the estate of a deceased person, which is discussed in more detail in chapter 15. Here it is enough to say that if your estate is worth less than £12,500 you will pay no duty at all, but if it is worth more than that the duty rises rapidly to a maximum of 80% of the total net value of your estate (the total value of everything you leave). If your estate is likely to be within the dutiable range on your death, you possibly should be thinking about some Estate Duty planning now.

Learn as much as you possibly can about the different taxes and what you may be liable to pay. Make sure you know the address of the particular tax office to which you must write.

WISEGUIDE

How taxes are administered and collected

The Chancellor's taxation recommendations for the year are outlined in his Budget speech usually early in April. If his proposals are approved, following debates in Parliament on the Finance Bill which contains the detailed proposals, they then

The law

become law in the Finance Act which usually goes through in July.

Administration

The assessment and collection of the taxes imposed by the annual Finance Act is the responsibility of the Board of Inland Revenue. The Chief Inspector of Taxes Branch of that department, with its head office in Somerset House in the Strand, is responsible for the *assessment* of direct taxation while the office of the Accountant and Comptroller General in Worthing, is the head office dealing with the *collection* side.

Chief Inspector of Taxes Branch

This branch consists of over 700 local tax offices each under the control of a District Inspector and two or more Tax Inspectors assisting him. These local offices deal with the day-to-day matters of direct taxation, issue and receipt of tax return forms, making assessments, issuing P.A.Y.E. (pay as you earn) coding notices and so on. The staff in the offices are also available to deal with queries raised by taxpayers either by correspondence or by calling at the tax office concerned.

The Chief Inspector's Branch, through local Inspectors of Taxes, applies the law as contained in the various Finance Acts and reports of cases decided by the Courts. Most of us come into contact with the Inspector of Taxes only through our P.A.Y.E. coding notices and the need to complete a tax return. Your code number is sent to your employer each year, so that he may make the correct deduction from your wages and, if your tax circumstances change during the year, an amended notice is issued to you and to your employer.

Accountant and Comptroller General

The collection of tax is actually carried out by Collectors of Taxes whose offices are spread throughout the country, and who are under the control of the Accountant and Comptroller General.

When assessments showing tax payable are issued by the Inspector of Taxes, the Collector of Taxes is notified. He then makes sure that the tax is collected on the appropriate date with interest added if it becomes overdue.

The Collector is not told how the tax payable is arrived at, and cannot deal with any queries relating to the amounts assessed – his job is simply to collect tax which is due and payable.

Surtax Office

Under the present system of personal taxation, surtax, which is an additional tax charged on higher incomes, is administered by the Surtax Office, at Thames Ditton, Surrey. There the amount of surtax is assessed and an assessment issued, and once the taxpayer has agreed the amount of his liability, payment must be made direct to the Accountant and Comptroller General in Worthing. Surtax is payable on January 1st in respect of the previous financial year which ends on April 5th.

WISEGUIDE

The tax administrators and collectors have a great deal of work to do. Make sure you go to the right department to deal with your particular case and remember to quote your reference number.

Your tax return

The Taxes Management Act 1970 sets out the law which gives the taxman the right to require you to make a "return" of your income. This means that you must send him details of *all* your sources of income and claim any allowances to which you think you are entitled.

There are three main types of return form:

- P1, which is the one which goes to most employees
- 11P, which is issued to higher-paid employees
- 11 which is issued annually to self-employed people and others who have more complicated incomes.

WISEGUIDE

You will probably get form P1, so concentrate on this next section.

Form P1

A. This form asks for details of your income for the financial year just ended and your claim for allowances for the current year. For instance, the form issued in April 1971 is described as a 1971–72 Return, but requires actually details of your income for 1970–71 (that is, the year ended April 5, 1971) and invites a claim for personal allowances for 1971–72 (that is, the year which will end on April 5, 1972).

B. You will not be asked for details of your wages or salary from your main job on this form, because that information will have been given to the tax office by your employer.

C. You are required to show details of any other earnings that you may have received and particulars of any other sources of income and the amount received from each source.

If you are a married man you are required to give details of your wife's income, if she is living with you, because her income is "deemed" to be yours for taxation purposes. The form has columns so that you may show your wife's income separate from yours. This is necessary to enable the Inspector to give you the correct allowances as explained later in the section on personal allowances.

WISEGUIDE

Make sure you do not omit *any* source of income from your tax return. Always enter gross (before tax) income.

Forms 11P and 11

Basically, these forms are the same as the form P1, but they ask for rather more detail and form 11 is drafted specifically to cover the case of a self-employed person. These forms also contain a column for including the unearned income of children under the age of 18 who are "not regularly working" since such income is taxed as if it were the income of the parent. (This is something which will shortly be modified.)

Separate Assessment

Although the law is that the income of a married woman living with her husband is treated as the income of her husband you may prefer to have your tax calculated separately. It must be emphasised that there is at present no tax advantage in separate assessment – all that happens is that the total tax bill is divided between you and your wife in proportion to your respective incomes and the tax is then claimed from each of you separately. The separate assessment of earned income which is to be introduced by the Finance Act 1971 is dealt with later, in the Tax and Marriage section.

WISEGUIDE

At present, married people have nothing to gain from separate assessment.

How to complete your tax return

The form sets out the various headings of income and there are detailed printed instructions issued as an inset to each form.

Points to bear in mind

A. Always enter the gross (before tax) amount received from each source of income – freelance, interest, dividends, etc. – rounding down to the nearest £.

B. If you have received no income from a particular source you write "None" in the appropriate space.

C. If you are completing a form P1 you do not need to show your earnings from the main source, but in the cases of forms 11P or 11 you should enter the gross amount shown by your employer in the *Certificate of Pay and Tax Deducted which he hands to you at the end of the tax year (form P60).*

D. Do *not* enter gifts of cash or kind which you have received from relatives or personal friends, or grants toward education costs.

E. Claim *all* reasonable expenses which have been incurred in connection with your employment.

F. It does not pay to omit anything from your returns. The tax-man has a first-class information service and the chances are that eventually he will find out that your returns have not been correct. When he does find out, you will have to pay not only the tax that you should have paid, but also interest on the amount, and probably a penalty as well.

G. Make sure that you claim *all* the allowances to which you are entitled and remember that the allowances are for the year ahead, not the year just ended as in the case of income.

H. You must remember to sign the Declaration on the front of the form and give the other information required by that part of the form.

I. Always keep a copy of your tax return.

Follow the points above very carefully.

WISEGUIDE

What is income?

No one has yet defined this in a way which satisfies everyone. Broadly, it is any money you receive as a reward for your labour, for providing facilities, for investing your capital; or the amount you receive from someone else under a legally binding agreement to pay you an annual sum, like a covenant, or maintenance for children.

Because income comes in so many different forms, the Tax Acts lay down a considerable number of rules relating to the manner in which the amount of income from each income-producing source is to be calculated. These rules are contained in the Acts in what are called *Schedules*.

There are six schedules, which are:

Schedule A: which deals with rents and other income from property (unless the property is let furnished)

Schedule B: income from woodlands run as a business

Schedule C: income from certain government and local authority stocks

Schedule D: this schedule is subdivided into Cases I to VI, and includes profits from trades, professions or vocations, income or interest from investments or annuities, income from abroad other than employment income and all other items of income not specifically covered by any of the other schedules and including, for instance, income from the furnished letting of property

Schedule E: income received from employment

Schedule F: concerns companies only.

If any money you get cannot be regarded as income within the rules as contained in the six schedules, it is not taxable and need not be shown as income in your return; for example, a privately-agreed maintenance payment. But it may be a capital gain and should be shown as such in the capital gains section of your return (see the section on Capital Gains for more information about such items).

Earnings are income (schedule E)

Obviously, earnings from your full-time job are income, and, unless you are completing a form P1, you should enter the gross amount that you earn for the year even if you do not receive part of your earnings until after the end of the year, like, say, commission paid later. In addition you must include the gross amount earned by your wife if you are a married man and, if either of you have any casual earnings, such as lecture fees, wages for part-time work, these must also be shown. Tips are income and so is anything you receive in kind from your employer such as goods, vouchers (except luncheon vouchers to a value not exceeding 15p) and, usually, rent-free accommodation.

Pensions and social security benefits are income (schedule E)

You must enter the full amount of a state retirement pension or a pension received from a previous employer, but certain types of pensions such as those received for wounds and disabilities, certain supplementary pensions and additional pensions for injuries suffered at work are exempt and need not be shown. Family allowances and widows' benefits and other social security benefits must be included with the exception of:

- Sickness and unemployment benefit.
- Maternity grant and maternity allowance.
- Death grant, and industrial injury benefits.
- Supplementary allowances.

Interest and dividends received are income (schedule D case III)

- Many people have a National Savings Bank Ordinary or Investment account or a Trustee Savings Bank Ordinary or Investment account. If this applies to you the full amount received or credited to your account in the tax year must be declared. On ordinary accounts (but not investment accounts) the first £21 of interest received each year is exempt but the total figure must be entered on your return. The Inspector will deduct the exempt portion and only include the balance in your assessment (see Chapter 2 on savings).

● If you have interest on other bank deposit accounts, it is taxable in full and you must enter the name of the bank and the full amount of the interest paid or credited in the tax year.

● Interest (not dividends on purchases) from Co-operative Societies and interest on Defence Bonds, War Loan and so on is taxable and you must enter the gross amount received.

● Interest on National Savings Certificates and interest and bonuses under the National Save as You Earn Scheme need not be entered.

● Tax on building society interest has been paid by the society, but you must enter the amount you receive because it is liable to surtax if your income is high enough.

● The gross amount of dividends received and the names of the paying companies concerned must be entered in your return. If there is insufficient room on the form prepare a separate list and enter only the total on the form. Send a copy of the list with your return. Income tax is paid on dividends before they come to you, but you may have to pay surtax on them.

If you receive a payment as a beneficiary of a trust or if you receive an annuity you should receive a form R185E or R185 giving details of the payment. In both cases tax of 38·75% will be deducted by the payer and paid to the Inland Revenue and may be credited to you against your total tax liability.

Payments from a trust and annuities are income (schedule D case III)

● Any money received from the letting or hiring of premises is taxable as income, but you are allowed to make certain deductions before reaching the final amount to be taxed.

Rents received for letting premises are income (schedule A or schedule D case VI)

● Enter the gross amount of rent received and the total of the expenses claimed and extend the difference into the income column for yourself or your wife as the case may be. The actual expenses claimed should be detailed in a statement attached to your return.

● If only part of the property is let you should only claim the expenses relative to the part let, making apportionments where necessary.

● You may receive a premium from the tenancy or you may receive rent in kind, for instance if your tenant agrees to carry out certain improvements to the property in lieu of rent. If this is the case, full details should be submitted with your return. *Remember that rents received for rooms in your own home which you have let are also income, and must be included in your return,*

Profits from a trade or business are income (schedule D cases I and II)

and so must rents for a garage or caravan site or similar property.

● You must prepare a statement to go with your return showing:
a) Your gross takings from sales, commission, services or other business income.
b) All the expenses you have incurred.

The basic rule is that all expenses "wholly and exclusively laid out or expended for the purposes of" the business are allowable except certain specified items such as structural alterations to business premises, and personal expenses and salaries of the proprietors of the business. The difference between your business income and allowable expenses may be a profit or a loss and should be entered in your return. Keep your income and expenses vouchers in case the Inspector asks to see them.

● The profit or loss to be entered in your return is that for your business year which ends in the tax year for which you are giving particulars of your income. This means that, for example, in completing your return for 1971-72 the results of a business year ended on December 31, 1970, will be entered as income of the year ended April 5, 1971.

● The rules relating to "assessments" (what you must pay, initially at least) on business income provide that the assessment for the tax year is based on the profit of the business year ending in the previous tax year. This is called "the preceding year basis". Thus your profit for the year ended December 31, 1970 is charged to tax for 1971–72. There are special rules applying to the opening and closing years of the business.

WISEGUIDE

Learn to know exactly what counts as income and keep all bills, receipts and details to prove your case to the taxman.

Expenses and outgoings

● You can claim the cost of tools or special clothes that you use at work in addition to any other expenses that you have to meet while you are working. Give full details either in the return or in an accompanying statement. You may not claim the cost of travel between home and work nor business entertainment unless you are entertaining an overseas customer.

● If you use your own car for business purposes you may claim some part of the cost of running the car, including wear and tear. Give the Inspector full particulars of the car, the total mileage in the year and the approximate amount of business mileage and he will calculate the allowance due. If you borrowed money to buy the car you may also be entitled to claim some of the interest which you pay on the loan.

● Superannuation contributions to an approved fund other than a trade union may be claimed and you may also claim fees or subscriptions to a professional body if the activities of the body are relevant to your work.

● Interest paid on a mortgage or loan obtained for a qualifying purpose is allowed as a deduction from your income. Examples of qualifying purposes are:

a) a mortgage to purchase your home or to make improvements to it

b) a loan to buy a large caravan which you will use as a home

c) money borrowed to invest in your business.

Make sure you claim for *all* the expenses to which you are entitled.

WISEGUIDE

The most recent addition to the information that you are required to show in your tax return relates to capital gains. You must give full details of "chargeable" assets acquired or disposed of and calculate the amount of the gain or loss on disposal.

Chargeable assets include almost any property, business or private, and rights over property with the following main exceptions:

a) Items of household goods and personal belongings worth less than £1,000 at the time of acquisition and disposal

b) Private cars, animals, caravans and boats

c) Savings certificates, premium bonds and certain other government securities

d) Life insurance policies

e) Gifts of assets totalling less than £100 in value in the year

f) Your principal private residence.

Calculating the gain

You "dispose" of an asset if you sell it, exchange it or give it away. Even if you give it to a relative or friend it is a "disposal" and you will have to pay tax on any gain by reference to the market value of the asset at the date of the gift.

Capital gains

The rules for calculating gains or losses on disposal are extensive and very complicated, but in general it may be said that you calculate a gain as follows:

a) Find out the *net* amount that you receive for the asset (proceeds less costs), or its market value at the date of disposal;

b) Find out the cost of the asset when you acquired it, including costs of acquisition. Add to this any further expenditure incurred in improving the asset.

c) Deduct (b) from (a) – the answer is the amount of the gain on disposal. If (b) is greater than (a) then you have a loss on disposal and may deduct it from a gain or carry it forward until you have one.

The gain is charged to tax at 30% or half of it is charged at your highest income tax and surtax rates if more beneficial. There are special rules where assets were acquired before April 6, 1965 or where only part of an asset has been disposed of but these are too detailed to be dealt with here.

WISEGUIDE

Unless you are an investor on the stock exchange, or own two houses, or invest in expensive antiques, etc., capital gains tax is unlikely to affect you.

Allowances against tax

Personal allowances

These are deducted from your gross income. The rest is taxed at 38·75%.

You may be entitled to claim some of the following allowances:

Earned income relief

This is a relief which is available if either you or your wife have earned income such as earnings, business income, pensions and family allowances.

The relief is 2/9ths of your joint earned incomes up to £4,005 and 15% of any amount above that level. It is not necessary to claim this relief in your tax return as it is given automatically.

Personal deduction

If you are unmarried, separated or divorced you are entitled to a deduction of £325. This is increased to £465 for a married man who has a wife living with him or who is completely maintained by him. If the marriage takes place during the tax year the increased allowance is reduced as explained in the section on Tax and Marriage.

Wife's earned income

If your wife is earning or self-employed a deduction of 7/9ths of her income may be claimed subject to a maximum of £325.

Children

The allowance is based upon the age of the child at the beginning of the tax year as follows:

- If over 16, £205
- If over 11 but not over 16, £180
- If not over 11 or born during the year, £155.

The allowance is given not only for your own children but for any other child of which you have the custody and maintain at your own expense.

Note: A child over sixteen for whom an allowance is claimed must be receiving full-time education at a recognised educational establishment or undergoing full-time training for a trade, profession or vocation for a period of not less than two years.

If the child has income in its own right, the allowance is reduced by one pound for each pound of income over £115, but the reduction does not apply to the income of a child under 18 who is "not regularly working" which is taxed as income of the parent.

If you are a parent in receipt of a family allowance your total personal allowances will be restricted by an amount (intended at £42 for 1971–72) for each family allowance received. This is to recover from you the ten shillings a week increase in the family allowance which came into effect in 1968.

WISEGUIDE

These are the basic personal allowances. Know them and claim them.

Other possible allowances

Read this section along with Chapter 8.

Life assurance

A deduction may be claimed for premiums paid by you or your wife on a "qualifying" policy which insures either your own or your wife's life.

A "qualifying policy", generally speaking, includes a life or endowment policy capable of running for ten years or more but there are a number of conditions which must be satisfied which should not affect the normal policy.

There are two restrictions to the relief which may be claimed.

First: the allowable yearly premium on each policy must not exceed 7% of the sum payable on death.

Second: the total allowable premiums may not exceed 1/6th of your total income for the year, that is, before deducting your personal allowances.

The relief is 2/5ths of the eligible premiums paid with a minimum of £10.

WISEGUIDE

Find out if a policy qualifies for relief *before* you take it out.

Housekeeper

● If you are a widow or widower and have a female relative resident with you or an unrelated female employed by and resident with you in the capacity of housekeeper you may claim an allowance of £75. The allowance may also be claimed if you are unmarried and have a female relative living with and maintained by you to look after a brother or sister or any child for whom the child allowance is available.

● If by reason of old age or infirmity you depend on the services of a resident daughter there is an allowance of £40.

● If you have a child for whom you claim child allowance and your wife is wholly incapacitated throughout the year or alternatively you are not entitled to the married allowance, you may claim an allowance of £100 provided you are not also entitled to the housekeeper allowance of £75.

Dependent relative

● This relief is £75 in respect of a dependent relative maintained by you who is incapacitated by old age or infirmity or is your widowed, divorced or separated mother or mother-in-law. If you are a woman other than a married woman living with your husband, the relief is increased to £110. If the dependant does not reside with you the allowance is based on the amount contributed, not exceeding the amount of the allowance. In either event the relief is reduced by £1 for every £1 of the dependant's income in excess of a certain limit (£289 for 1971–72).

WISEGUIDE

Some people who are eligible do not claim these allowances – check your position.

Persons aged 65 or over

If you or your wife are 65 or over at any time during the tax year the following provisions may apply to you.

A) Age exemption:
If your total income for 1971–72 does not exceed £504 if you are single or £786 if you are married you pay no tax. For 1972–73 these limits will be raised to £530 and £825 respectively. If your total income is slightly in excess of these levels marginal relief will be given.

B) Age allowance:
If your total income, if you are single, does not exceed £1,000

or your joint total income, if married, does not exceed £1,200, a 2/9ths deduction from that income, whether earned or investment income, may be claimed. Marginal relief is available where your total income is slightly in excess of this limit.

C) *Small income relief:*

If your total income, from all sources, does not exceed £450, you may claim a 2/9ths deduction against all your income whether earned or not. Where your income is above £450 but below £750 marginal relief is available.

D) *Blind person's allowance:*

A registered blind person may claim an allowance of £100 reduced by 7/9ths of any disability receipts for the year. If both husband and wife are blind the allowance is £200 less 7/9ths of any disability receipts.

If you are over 65 you probably need all the tax relief you can get. Check your position.

WISEGUIDE

Deliberate omission of any income from your return is illegal and is known as *tax evasion*. This is not the same as *tax avoidance*, which is reducing your tax liabilities by legal means.

Tax *avoidance* can be either deliberate or accidental. For example, anyone who on getting married claims the higher married person's allowance is indulging in a form of tax avoidance. His tax bill will usually be reduced without increasing that of his wife. The subject of tax and marriage is dealt with separately at the end of this chapter.

You do not have to be a top rate surtax payer to be able to benefit from tax planning, though obviously if you are, the possibilities for tax avoidance are greater than if you are not liable to surtax.

What are the legitimate possibilities for reducing your tax bill?

It is no use being entitled to tax reliefs if you do not tell your Inspector of Taxes about them. If you do not receive a tax return form and wish to claim allowances not previously claimed (you may do this within six years) ask the Inspector to send you one. If your circumstances change during the year, write to the Inspector immediately and tell him about it so that he can take the appropriate action. When you get a tax return check the allowances section with the notes and make sure that you have claimed all the allowances to which you are entitled. If in doubt

Cutting your tax bill

Claim all your allowances

A Practical Example

To illustrate the way in which the various items of income are assessed and personal allowances granted we will now look at the case of Mr. C. Lyon and see how much tax he might be expected to pay for the tax year 1971-72. Mr. Lyon works in the centre of a city and commutes each day from his home in the country. His wife has for some years run a small antique shop in the village and they have two children aged 10 and 15. Mrs. Lyon's widowed mother lives with them and her only income is her widow's state pension.

Mr. Lyon provided the following details of their joint income as follows:

Mr Lyon

(a) Salary £5,000 pa

(b) Post Office Savings Bank interest —ordinary account £15

Mrs Lyon

(c) Antique business—taxable profit for 12 months to December 31st, 1970 £490

(d) Family allowance £46

Their expenses amounted to:

Mr Lyon

(e) Season ticket to his office £150

(f) Premium on life policy on own life providing for £2,000 with profits after 10 years or on earlier death £145

(g) Interest to building society on house mortgage £400

(h) Contribution to firm's pension scheme £250

Mrs Lyon

(i) Retirement annuity premium £60

(j) Cost of home help £140

(k) Premium on children's endowment policy maturing at age 21 £15

Points to bear in mind

The **Post Office Savings Bank** interest on ordinary account is below £21 and therefore exempt from tax.

The **profits** from the antique business are assessable on the "preceding year" basis and the £490 is therefore assessable for 1971-72. Since this is wife's earned income the seven-ninths wife's earned income allowance may be claimed, maximum £325.

The **family allowance** qualifies as earned income but total personal allowances must be cut back by £42

The cost of **travel** between home and work is not allowed.

The **allowable premium** is restricted to 7 per cent x £2,000 = £140.

There is no allowance for the cost of **home help** as Mrs. Lyon is not incapacitated through the whole of the tax year.

Relief may be claimed only in respect of policies on the life of Mr. or Mrs. Lyon.

The calculations of Mr. Lyon's anticipated tax liability for 1971-72 proceeds as follows:

Mr Lyon

Salary	£5,000
Less pension fund contributions	250
	4,750

Mrs Lyon

Profits from antique business	£490	
Less retirement annuity premium	60	
		430
Family allowance		46
		5,226
Less Interest paid to building society		400
		4,826

Personal allowances

Earned income relief —		
2/9ths x £4,005		£890
15% x 821		123
£4,826		£1,013
Personal deduction (married)		465
Wife's earned income allowance (maximum)		325
Children (£155 + £180)		335
Dependent relative		75
Life Assurance 2/5ths x £140		56
		2,269
Less restriction		42
		2,227
		£2,599

Tax payable £2,599 x 38.75 per cent* = £1,007.11

* £38.75 per cent is the present "standard rate" of income tax.

ask the Inspector.

Get as large a mortgage as possible

The interest you pay on a mortgage is eligible for tax relief whilst interest paid on other loans, such as to buy a car, may not be. It pays to borrow as much as you can for the purchase of your house, leaving any spare cash available to purchase other items or to invest.

Remember, the rate of interest payable on a building society mortgage is usually lower than on other types of loan, such as from a finance house or for hire purchase. Your only opportunity to obtain this form of loan comes when you buy a house, so make the most of it while you can (see Chapter 6).

Use of life assurance for saving

If you intend to save regularly it will be well worth your while to save through life assurance, especially if you are young. You could combine this with an investment in a unit trust by taking out a unit-linked life assurance policy. See Chapter 13 on unit-linked assurance.

Benefits in kind

If you are employed it will usually be more beneficial to receive a benefit in kind from your employer rather than an increase in salary. Such a benefit can take the form of an interest-free mortgage, or a company car. You have obtained a benefit the cost of which to you is the tax payable on it.

Pension contributions

Whether you are employed or self-employed, contributions for approved pension benefits are deductible from your taxable income. This gives you a subsidised method of providing for your retirement.

Use of your home as an office

If you are a self-employed person and use part of your home for business purposes you may claim an appropriate part of the expenses of heating, lighting, rates, etc. as a business expense. However, if you set aside a specific part of your home as an office you will lose the private residence exemption for capital gains tax on that part of your property.

Tax and marriage

Although tax savings may not be one of the things a young man has in mind when he proposes to a young woman, nevertheless, it is in this area that the most simple and effective tax planning can be carried out.

Date of marriage

● If you marry early in the tax year your married personal allowance for that year will be higher than if you marry later. So even if tax is not your guiding light in fixing the day, it should at least be borne in mind!

However, your increased personal allowance is not the only tax consequence of marriage.

This is important

● In the year in which you marry, your wife is treated as *two* separate individuals for tax purposes. Up to the date of marriage she receives a full single person's allowance against her taxable income for that period. So her earnings up to £418 in that period will be exempt from tax. From date of marriage there is also the

Earnings		Total tax liability	
		As two single people	As a married couple
Bill	£1,000	£351	£296
Marjorie	£1,000		
Bill	£2,000	£954	£899
Marjorie	£2,000		
Bill	£4,000	£1,556	£1,626
Marjorie	£2,000		
Bill	£6,000	£2,605	£3,119
Marjorie	£3,000		
Bill	£15,000	£7,864	£8,961
Marjorie	£3,000		

From 1972-73 it is proposed that a married couple may elect to be assessed as two single people on their earnings. This means that they will receive only two single person's allowances in return for relinquishing the husband's married allowance and the extra allowance for the wife's earnings. In the example above, Marjorie and Bill would be advised to start thinking of being taxed as single people if they expect their joint earnings to be over £6,000 for a long time. Any investment income will still be treated as the husband's for tax purposes.

additional allowance equal to 7/9ths of your wife's earnings (maximum allowance £325). So, effectively there are two allowances to be set off against her earnings for the year. However, you do not get two allowances against your income. You receive only the married man's allowance of £465 less 1/12th of £140 (the difference between the single and married allowance) for each complete month of the tax year which has elapsed before the date of marriage.

If your wife intends to carry on working after marriage, it is important to choose the date of marriage carefully to make the best use of her two allowances.

WISEGUIDE

If a wife is earning less than £418 a year (£8 a week) she is not taxable in any event and the date is therefore irrelevant. Between £418 and £836 a year (£8 and £16 a week) there should be no more than £418 income in each broken period to obtain full advantage.

Over £836 a year (£16 a week) the aim should be to earn at least £418 in each period.

In certain circumstances, where both husband and wife are earning, they pay more tax than they would as single people, hence the expression, "it is cheaper to live in sin".

To illustrate this the table shows the total tax liabilities of two people, Bill and Marjorie, with various specimen incomes. It compares the position when they are single with that when they are married with no children and no commitments other than each other!

Self-employed husband

If you are self-employed and your wife does not work, one method of saving tax is to employ your wife in the business and pay her a reasonable, though not excessive, sum for her services. This will enable you to claim the wife's extra earned income allowance which otherwise would not be available.

WISEGUIDE

You *cannot avoid* paying tax, but by careful study you *can reduce* your tax burden.

Chapter 17

The Law

Most chapters in this book have referred to the legal aspects of saving and spending money in one form or another. This chapter re-emphasises and explains the legal implications involved in monetary transactions.

Unlike many financial institutions, such as banks and finance houses which use money all the time but are not actually defined in law, money actually has a legal existence and definition.

What money is

Money, as an entity, includes bank-notes as well as coins. It can also include the amount standing to your credit in a bank account.

The uses of money

The advantage of money is that it facilitates exchange because it is divided into units, e.g. pounds and pence which are commonly accepted and readily transferable.

Points to watch

● Today gold coin is no longer legal currency, and

● Bank notes are regarded as cash.

A bank note is nothing more than the bank's written promise to pay a sum of money. This can only be issued by the Bank of England. If you read the wording on a bank note you will see that it says "I promise to pay the bearer on demand the sum of one pound". This is signed by the Chief Cashier on behalf of the Governor and Company of the Bank of England.

● In other words, bank notes are legal tender.

In law, the bank is simply promising to pay one pound to anyone who presents the note for payment. We are not entitled to ask for gold coin in exchange for the bank note, but only for cupro-nickel *pieces*.

If someone owes us a debt, he can give us a cheque or a promissory note in payment. Bank notes, promissory notes and cheques are examples of negotiable instruments (see chapter 4 on bank accounts).

Know exactly what money is and what you can and cannot do with it.

WISEGUIDE

In English law it is the *time of payment* of a debt which is important *not the date when the agreement is signed*. For example, an agreement to pay £100 may be followed by a devaluation of the £1. Nevertheless, the payment is to be made in pounds as devalued on the International Currency Market and not at the value of the pounds before devaluation.

Paying debts

WISEGUIDE

When you are paying a debt you should pay the amount stated on the bill without adjustments for changes in international money rates.

Owing money

There are many rules of law governing the position of a person who owes money.

● The creditor (the person to whom the money is owed) commits an offence if he harasses or sends out threatening letters to frighten the debtor (the person who owes the money) into making payments. These letters are sometimes known as "blue frighteners", because they are intended to make the debtor think that they are a court summons.

● The creditor commits a criminal offence if he makes any threat, e.g. that he will tell other persons some discreditable fact about the debtor. He may not put any pressure on the debtor beyond asking for payment, and if payment is not made, by taking the case to court.

● If a debtor feels that he is being unjustly hounded by the creditor, his best course is to report the matter to the police.

What is legal tender?

This means the creditor is entitled to be paid in cash. The money must be actually produced and offered to the creditor, or one of his employees. The creditor is not obliged to accept a cheque or any payment in an unusual way. If you owe someone £50 you cannot *insist* in their accepting a suitcase containing 5,000 new pence in copper as this would *not* amount to legal tender.

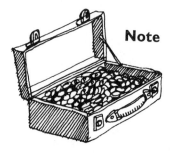

Note All bank notes are legal tender in England and Wales, but the number of coins which need be accepted as legal tender is limited.

In theory the debtor must offer the precise amount he owes. The creditor is not obliged to have change ready, but in practice he will generally be only too pleased to receive his money and will always give change. If he has no change available and the debtor refuses to hand over the exact amount of money there is no legal tender of the debt.

WISEGUIDE

If the creditor brings a court action for the amount owed, he would not be entitled to any legal costs or expenses if he had previously refused legal tender.

● Once legal tender of the debt has been made the creditor cannot claim further interest on the debt beyond that date.

Applying payments to particular debts

It is the law that if someone owes another person several sums of money in respect of different matters, he must make it clear when making a payment which particular debt he is paying.

An example: You may owe money to a retailer for, say, a television, a radio and a washing machine, all held on hire-purchase. If you have paid more than a third in respect of the television and radio the dealer cannot take them back without a court order. But you may owe £10 short of one third on the washing machine and the dealer could then take it back. If you go into the shop to make payment of the £10, you should specify that it relates to the washing machine. If you do this, it cannot be reclaimed by the dealer. If you do not make this clear, the creditor has the right to put it to any of your debts as he thinks fit. If he credits the payment to your television account, he could, if he chooses, take back the washing machine.

When goods can be kept by the dealer

This is also best explained by an example:

A woman may take several dresses to a dry-cleaner for cleaning or repair. She may suddenly find that she has no money at hand to pay the charges and she desperately needs a particular dress to go to her daughter's wedding. If she offers to pay the dry-cleaner the charges owing on the particular dress, he cannot retain it and must hand it over. He can only keep the dresses for which his charges have not been paid.

Liens

This right of retention is known in law as a *lien*. Anyone who does work on someone else's goods has this right to hold them until his charges have been paid, whether he is a shoe repairer or a garage mechanic.

Examples:

You cannot insist on having your car back until you have paid for the work done on it. If you go into the garage and take it without the garage owner's consent, you are committing a criminal offence.

Other persons who have the right of lien are solicitors, stock-brokers, bankers and auctioneers. It should be noted that their right is called a general lien. They can keep *any* valuables or documents or articles which may have come into their possession until all the debts to them have been paid.

A solicitor may have defended someone on a driving charge in the Magistrates' Court, but not been paid his fee of £30. He may also hold other documents belonging to his client which the client urgently needs, e.g. the Title Deeds to his house. Even though the client has paid all the charges in relation to his house, he cannot have those documents until he has also paid the outstanding fee of £30.

A bank similarly has the right to keep any securities or valuables which a customer has deposited with it, until the customer has cleared his overdraft.

WISEGUIDE

Pay your debts unless you wish to surrender the goods or services involved.

Sending money by post

If you send a payment through the post, this will be at your own risk. The risk of its being lost in the post would lie with your creditor only if he specifically asked for the money to be posted. Hence many creditors prefer to call on the debtor to collect payment in cash.

Actual sums of money should be sent by registered post – not by recorded delivery. If you send a cheque it is wise to mark it "not negotiable", so that only the payee can cash it. It is also a good idea to use a postal order because in law this is not negotiable either. This means that if it is lost and the counterfoil has been retained, the money can be reclaimed, even though some unauthorised person has found it and cashed it.

WISEGUIDE

Money can be safely sent through the post if you do it the right way. Don't run the risk of losing it. Always send a covering letter, state the account number and keep a copy of your letter.

Payments made by mistake

If money is paid because of some mistake, it can usually be claimed back, but it is important that the mistake be one of fact. Any payment made owing to a mistake of law cannot be recovered.

Points to watch

When making any payment it is wise to preserve the receipt for six years. (There is now no longer any need for a stamp on a receipt, no matter how large the sum.) After six years the right to claim any debt is barred as a matter of law, unless there is some admission of the debt in writing in the meantime, or a payment has been made on account. The six years runs from the date of the last payment made towards the debt.

Take care

If a creditor writes to claim repayment of a forgotten debt after more than six years, it is wise not to reply in writing but to consult a solicitor. Even after six years, a written acknowledgement, if signed, may operate to revive the debt.

Court judgements

In contrast, if money is owed under a court judgement, the creditor's right to claim the money lasts twelve years.

The duty to prove payment

● Anyone who admits a debt was once owing, may be forced to pay it a second time unless he can *prove* that he has already paid it.

● It is sensible to preserve any written receipt or acknowledgement from the creditor. This may be important if you pay money to a person who dies soon after. His relatives will not know that he has received the money, and unless you can show some letter from the deceased acknowledging payment, you may be forced to pay again.

Proof

If an independent witness was present when you paid over the money, his evidence would probably satisfy a judge. The best and simplest proof would be a signed letter of acknowledgement.

WISEGUIDE

Always get, and keep, receipts of payments.

Payment under protest

It may sometimes happen that one objects strenuously to paying, but has no choice, for example, because the bailiffs threaten to take away the furniture if payment is not made on the spot. In this case it should be made clear that payment is made "under protest".

Remember

1. If you can prove that the money was demanded without any legal right it can be claimed back and damages may be allowed as well.

2. You can claim back money you have been tricked into paying.

Blackmail

Unlawful claims to money are sometimes cloaked with the pretence of a commercial transaction. For example, a pretended journalist may offer to sell "a story" and the other person may be compelled to buy it because it contains some disreputable disclosures about him. The threat is that if he does not buy "the story", the other will sell it to a newspaper for publication. This amounts to demanding money by menaces and the police should be informed.

WISEGUIDE

Blackmail is a crime. Do not submit to it. Go to the police and you will be protected.

Receipts mistakenly sent

A new computer owned by a finance company may go hay-wire and send receipts to people who have in fact not paid. These receipts do not entitle them to avoid payment if it is later found that they were sent out in error and that no money had in fact come in. Alternatively, it could be proved that the money had been mistakenly credited to the wrong account, e.g. to the account of B. Jones instead of R. Jones.

WISEGUIDE

Check all your transactions because people to whom you owe money are not bound by "computer errors".

Transferring debts

Contrary to popular belief, debts can easily be transferred. If Dick is owed £100 by Tom, he can transfer this debt to Harry, who can then insist on payment by Tom.

To make this transfer valid in law, two things are necessary:

● The transfer to Harry should be in writing and signed by Dick.

● Harry should write to Tom (the debtor) to tell him the debt has been transferred. Once he has received this notice Tom cannot legally refuse to pay Harry and Dick drops out of the picture.

Remember

It is no concern of Tom's that Harry has not paid Dick anything for the transfer.

Transfer of liabilities

Liabilities are not the same as debts, and cannot be transferred to anyone else unless the creditor agrees. If the debtor gives a cheque in payment he is not transferring liability to the bank: he is merely ordering the bank to make payment on his behalf.

If there are no funds in his account and the bank does not honour the cheque, the debtor is still liable, not the bank. However, if the bank fails to meet a cheque when there is money in the account, this would be a serious matter and the bank would be liable to pay damages.

WISEGUIDE

Know your rights and responsibilities as far as debts are concerned.

Points to notice

It is important to remember that the transfer of assets such as shares, insurance policies, or the goodwill of a business or the copyright in a book, should always be by written document. Similarly the transfer of any interest in land or buildings *must* always be in writing if it is to be effective in law.

Lending money while on holiday and business abroad

A dangerous business. This can be dangerous because while one is abroad the loan would be governed by the law of that country. To avoid this insist on being given a cheque drawn on an English bank. This will mean that the loan is governed by English law.

It is very unwise to get involved in any financial transactions abroad without consulting a reputable lawyer there.

The complexity of arrangements which involves foreign law can be seen from the following example:

A man named Brook was on holiday in Monte Carlo and borrowed some money from a friend to play roulette. When he got back to England, Brook welshed on his debt. He said (quite rightly) that a loan for gambling was against English law, and so he need not repay it.

The English court held that as the loan was made in Monte Carlo it was subject to the law of Monaco (not English law) and that gambling was lawful in Monaco. The court in England ordered Brook to repay the money. Loans for gambling are against the law in England and need not be repaid.

Since the Gaming Act of 1968 it is lawful for a gambling club to accept a cheque provided cash or chips are given in exchange. Even though the club is licensed for gaming, it cannot accept post dated cheques.

The procedure in the High Court is very complicated. Creditors know this and often take proceedings in the High Court relying on the fact that the debtor does not know how to deal with the documents.

● The best course for the debtor is to write to the High Court and apply for the case to be transferred to the County Court. This can best be done by a solicitor.

● If you admit that you owe the money, write to the Court promptly and say this. Also give the Court full information about your financial position – both income and liabilities – and offer to pay weekly or monthly instalments. If the case is brought in the County Court you will be sent a special form on which you can state all this information.

● If you dispute the claim, you should *not* give this information but fill in the part of the form headed "Defence". Here you should set out the full reasons *why* you dispute the claim. For example, if you are sued for damage to a motor car, you could state that the accident was due to the carelessness of the other driver, e.g. in failing to signal that he was changing lanes.

Part admissions can be very useful if you admit *part* of the debt only. For example, a builder may claim £100 for work done when in fact it can be proved that the value of the work was only £50. The best course here is to pay into Court £50 "in full settlement".

The builder then has a choice. He can:

● Accept £50 and call it a day or

● Refuse the settlement and press his claim for the whole £100.

If you can call another builder to give evidence that the work was worth only £50, the judge will probably accept that you have been overcharged and give judgement for £50 only. In this case you would be entitled to be paid *all* your legal costs and out of pocket expenses, such as loss of time and travelling to attend court and also your witness's expenses. In other words, the builder, although entitled to be paid £50, might find that most of it is used up in paying *your* legal costs and expenses.

WISEGUIDE

Payment into Court is something of a gamble because if the builder succeeded in convincing the judge that the work done was worth, say, £60, i.e. £10 *more* than you had paid into Court, you would then have to pay all *his* costs and expenses.

Interest on judgements

Sometimes it may be of benefit to a debtor if judgement is entered against him. For example, if the borrower owes £500 and has agreed to pay 20% interest per year, the rate of interest is reduced to 4% once judgement is given. But this applies only in the High Court. After judgement is given in the County Court, *no* interest at all is payable.

The right to claim interest on a debt or damages for an injury

It was once thought that it was improper to claim interest on a private debt if the debtor was late in repaying it. Interest was payable only if a specific rate of interest had been agreed in the first place, in other words, if it was a moneylending or commercial transaction. In fact the law was changed only as recently as 1934. Now, if you lend a friend £100 for 2 weeks and he takes 2 years to pay it back, you are entitled to interest on your money for the whole of the 2 years. This is common sense, because if you had put your money in the National Savings Bank or a Building Society you would have got interest on it.

The rate of interest a court will allow is usually about 5% a year, but a judge may allow interest at as much as 1% above the current bank rate.

Even on a claim for damages, you are entitled to be paid interest. If you are knocked down by a car and have to bring a protracted court action, this may take several years before judgement is given in your favour. When a judge awards the injured person, say, £5,000 damages for a broken leg and general pain and suffering he can add to it interest at the current bank rate.

Interest is calculated for the whole of the period from the date of the accident until the date of the judgement. The point is that the person injured in fact became entitled to compensation immediately after the date of his injury. The fact that, owing to the law's delays, he does not receive payment until years later, is not *his* fault. If he had been paid promptly he could have invested the money in a Building Society and received interest on it.

WISEGUIDE

If you are entitled to interest on a debt, make sure you get it.

Liability for giving misleading information

There are many provisions in the Companies Acts to prevent prospective investors being cheated or misled. These regulations are enforced by the Criminal Courts through the police and their details need not concern the average investor. When buying shares it is important for the investor to have expert advice from a reputable person.

Protection for investors

The Government protects all investors.

First: Anyone dealing in shares or securities must be licensed as a dealer by the Department of Trade and Industry.

Second: It should be remembered that anyone who attempts to persuade another person to invest money should be very careful what he says. If he makes a statement or promise knowing it to be false or misleading, or if he dishonestly conceals any material facts, he is liable to long term imprisonment.

Third: Investors on the Stock Exchange should make sure that they are given a *written contract note* setting out the particulars of the shares bought.

WISEGUIDE

You may be entitled to compensation for misleading information. Find out if you are.

Ending up in "Carey Street"

The bankruptcy court used to be in Carey Street but is now in Victory House, Kingsway.

A personal application

If you are hopelessly in debt and see no possible way of repayment, bankruptcy may be the only way out. This often happens when a business man guarantees repayment of a debt owed by a company, never thinking that he himself might one day be called upon to pay up if the company defaults.

In this case, all he needs is the sum of £10 to file his own Petition. Once he is made bankrupt he is released from all his debts and liabilities. After that he can get a job and need concern himself only with providing for himself and his family.

A creditor's petition

It is also open to any creditor who is owed more than £50 to file a Petition asking that the debtor be declared bankrupt. This is a complicated procedure and is usually done by solicitors.

Points to watch

● Before a Petition can be filed, the debtor is usually sent a document called a Bankruptcy Notice. This demands payment of the amount owed within 7 days. If it is not paid the creditor can file a Petition.

● The Petition must be handed to the debtor personally unless it can be proved that he is avoiding receiving it. It notifies him of the date on which he must attend Court. From the debtor's point of view the danger of avoiding receipt of the Petition is that it may be posted. If he does not receive it, he may not know the court date and so will not be able to attend to plead with the judge not to make him bankrupt.

● If the judge finds he is hopelessly in debt, he will make a receiving Order. Although the debtor is not yet legally bankrupt this Order transfers all his possessions and property to the Official Receiver. The Official Receiver will send an Inspector to close down any business run by the debtor and take control of any assets. The Inspector then begins a full investigation of the debtor's financial affairs.

● He has extremely wide powers to question not only the debtor but also his family and business connections. If the debtor refuses to obey the Inspector, he can apply to the judge to have the debtor sent to prison.

WISEGUIDE

Going Bankrupt can have advantages, but take care – you may end up in jail if you do not obey the Court's ruling. Read the next section carefully.

The job of the Receiver

The Official Receiver must first prepare a full statement of the debtor's financial affairs. This is based largely on the debtor's own statement of affairs which he is bound in law to give.

All creditors are entitled to have a copy of the statement of affairs, and eventually a meeting of creditors is called.

The disadvantages

● Unless the creditors are prepared to accept the debtor's proposal to pay by instalments he will be made bankrupt. This is serious because a bankrupt *virtually loses his status as a free man.* In fact he is treated almost as a criminal and can be guilty of a large number of criminal offences which do not apply to ordinary people.

Example: the most common offence is when a debtor tries to obtain credit for more than £10 and does not disclose that he is an undischarged bankrupt. He can also be sent to prison if he starts in business again under another name without disclosing that he is still an undischarged bankrupt.

● The most important aspect of bankruptcy is that it deters a debtor from running up debts rashly. Thus when he comes before the court he is publicly questioned as to the reasons for his insolvency. He will be liable to prosecution if it becomes clear that he has wilfully increased the amount for which he is in debt.

On the other hand, if he has not been at fault, but his bankruptcy is due to a simple business failure, the court may discharge him from bankruptcy, even though he cannot pay all he owes. He can then start in business again with a clean slate.

WISEGUIDE

There is nothing basically dishonourable in being made bankrupt. It has happened to some successful business men, and they have been able to put it behind them and start again.

Bankruptcy and creditors

As well as being of immense help to the debtor it can also benefit the creditors. When a man is made bankrupt those assets which he still has are frozen. They are taken by his Trustee in bankruptcy, sold, and anything that is left over is shared among all the creditors. They may not be paid in full but from their point of view it is not always a total loss. At least something can often be salvaged from the shipwreck, for example, 50p for each pound owed, which is better than nothing.

The legal aspects of lending

Lending money to friends in business

It can be dangerous to lend money to someone for a business venture if the rate of interest goes up as the profits increase. In this case, the person lending the money may be held liable as a partner if the business subsequently gets into debt. To escape liability in this case the person lending the money must make it very clear in a *written agreement* that no partnership is intended. If in law he is held to be a partner, he will not only lose the loan he has made to the business, but will have to contribute from his own pocket any loss that the business has made. Although he may be entitled to be repaid all the money by the person who ran it, this right may be of little use if this person has no money.

The dangers of partnership

Similarly entering into a trading partnership, even as a sleeping partner, can be dangerous because the other partners have authority to borrow money in the firm's name and obtain credit in other ways. Here again, if the partnership makes a loss, the sleeping partner may be saddled with it.

WISEGUIDE

If you are thinking of lending money or taking part in a business venture, always go and see a solicitor first. It is always worth the expense involved in getting proper documents drawn up.

How much can they charge?

When a solicitor does work for you his charges are mostly fixed by law. Some fees are fixed by reference to scales e.g. when buying or renting property you pay according to the money or rent involved.

House buying

When you buy a house, the fee your solicitor will charge is geared exactly to the cost of the house. The more expensive the house the higher his fee will be.

A warning

When you sell a house you can use an estate agent to find a buyer. His fee is much higher than the solicitor's fee. If he cannot find a buyer he cannot claim any payment or any reimbursement for his expenses.

The solicitor on the other hand is still entitled to be paid something for any work he has done despite the fact that the sale or purchase falls through (see also chapter 5).

When you decide to buy a house it is a good rule not to pay any money to the estate agent. Sometimes the agent will ask you to pay a small deposit, say £25, to show your good faith, but it is always safer to pay the deposit to a solicitor. Usually one tenth of the purchase price e.g. £500 on a £5,000 house is paid when you sign the contract. This binds you to go ahead with the purchase. It is advisable to pay this to your own solicitor. He can then pay it over to the seller's solicitor who will hold it as stake-holder. Do not sign any document unless your solicitor tells you to do so. If before this you have to write to the agent or owner, head all letters "subject to contract".

Selling your house

If, when you sell your home you employ an estate agent, remember you may be held responsible for his actions. For example, a prospective buyer may be talked into paying him a deposit. If the estate agent makes off with the money you will have to repay it to the buyer.

Pay your solicitor in preference to an estate agent if possible.

Costs in court actions

If you win, your legal costs (or most of them) will be paid by the loser. If you lose, you will have to pay your own costs and the winner's costs too – not a very bright prospect.

The costs will be set out on a bill and you or your solicitor will be sent a copy. A date is then fixed for the bill to be compared by a court official with the list of permitted charges. You or your solicitor are entitled to go along and object to any items which appear too high.

WISEGUIDE

Court costs can be high. Don't go to court unless you are fairly sure of winning.

How solicitors charge clients

Usually a solicitor asks the client to pay him a sum of money on account of costs. When the case is over he will send the client a bill for the work actually carried out.

The bill will give a short summary of the case with a fee at the end. His proposed charge must be fair and reasonable. This will depend on the importance and complexity of the matter, the number of documents prepared and the time actually spent on it by the solicitor. If you think you are being overcharged you can ask for a more detailed bill. This will list every item of work done and show a charge for it.

WISEGUIDE

If you don't think your solicitor's bill is fair, ask your solicitor's professional body (the Law Society in Chancery Lane, WC2) to check it.

● If you are still dissatisfied you may as a last resort go to court and ask them to decide what is a fair and reasonable fee.

Solicitors' charges generally

When a solicitor acts on a divorce or defends someone on a driving charge he may fix a fee in advance. If so, he is still entitled to his full fee although the client eventually decides not to pursue the case.

If a client has no money to pay legal fees, e.g. a wife deserted by her husband, she can ask the solicitor to give her forms to apply for free legal aid. This will take about a month, but if legal aid is granted the Government will pay the solicitor's bill.

WISEGUIDE

See if you are eligible for legal aid.

Paying by cheque
The advantage

A cheque can be used in court to prove that you have made the payment. It is not necessary to have a separate receipt, although the debtor is entitled to one if he wants it. Incidentally, receipts no longer require to be stamped.

A creditor is not obliged to accept a cheque but can insist on payment by cash. This is because it is not always certain that the bank will meet a cheque. There may be no funds in the account or the person giving the cheque may change his mind and stop payment.

WISEGUIDE

Once a cheque is written and signed and handed over the debtor is liable for that sum. Stopping a cheque does not release him from liability.

Post-dated cheques

It is often useful to give a post-dated cheque: for example, if you are buying a second hand washing machine, a post-dated cheque may afford a certain protection in case the machine is not delivered. Alternatively you may find that the machine is not in working order although the seller guaranteed that it was working. In either case by giving a post-dated cheque you have sufficient time to stop payment. It would be up to the seller to sue you on the cheque. You must then raise a counter-claim that the seller has broken his guarantee or failed to supply the machine.

The danger of giving a post-dated cheque and stopping it is that the seller may transfer the cheque to a third person. In that case the third person would be entitled to sue you on the cheque and you would have to pay it.

To stop the cheque being transferred it is possible to write on it the words "Account Payee only", and also the words "Not negotiable". The cheque should also be crossed, i.e. with two parallel lines straight down across the face of the cheque. It is not necessary to add the words "and Co", although this is often done in practice.

If you do all this the cheque cannot be transferred and no one else can get the benefit of it if it is lost or stolen.

WISEGUIDE

Post-dated cheques can give you protection, but make sure you fill them in properly.

Stopping a cheque

First: Telephone the bank and give them the date and number of the cheque and name of the payee.

Second: Confirm in writing. A bank will not stop a cheque unless it has very clear instructions to do so, because if it wrongly fails to honour a cheque when there is money in the customer's account the bank would be liable for damage to the customer's reputation, especially if the customer were in trade or business.

Lost cheque books
Losing a cheque book is a serious matter, and the bank should be notified immediately, and also the police.

Points to watch
● If a stranger forges your name on a cheque and the bank pays it, thinking it is your usual signature, you are not liable. It is the bank that will lose for paying on a cheque without authorisation.

● If a cheque is altered after it has been signed, e.g. the name of the payee is changed or the amount is increased, again the owner of the account is not liable to pay.

● The customer is liable only if he had carelessly left a gap or failed to insert the amount in words which would render alteration easy.

● It is highly dangerous to assign a blank cheque. If it has to be done it should be crossed and marked "Not negotiable". Also words such as "not exceeding ten pounds" should be written clearly across the cheque in case it gets into the wrong hands.

● It is well to remember that when writing out a cheque you must take precautions to prevent a possible forgery. This can be done by closing all gaps with a double line and adding "only" to the amount to be paid, e.g. "fifty pounds only".

WISEGUIDE

Read the above with chapter 4 on bank accounts.

Hire purchase and credit agreements
Distinguish carefully between these two types of instalment buying as discussed fully in chapter 3. A hire purchase agreement has completely different effects in law from a credit sale agreement.

Credit sales
What is bought on credit sale belongs to the purchaser from the moment it is delivered. It can be re-sold if the buyer wishes. If it is re-sold the whole of the unpaid balance may have to be repaid immediately. Read the Agreement to see whether this is the case.

Credit sale agreements are usually very short documents but they contain one important provision. *If the buyer defaults on even one instalment, he is liable to pay the whole of the balance outstanding.* The object of this provision is to permit the credit company to sue for the whole balance at once. Otherwise they would have to wait until the last instalment became due or alternatively sue for each instalment as it fell due.

Hire purchase
What is bought on hire purchase does not belong to the purchaser until the very last instalment is paid. The important point is that the goods belong to the hire purchase finance company and they can take them back if he defaults. The purchaser is not permitted to sell them. If he does, he may end up in a Magistrates' Court charged with theft.

But, once one third of the total price is paid, the hire purchase

company must apply to the county court if it wants the goods back.

In contrast the customer can *ask* the hire purchase company to take goods back and provided he has looked after them reasonably well not more than one half of the total price can be charged. If there are more instalments outstanding than this, the customer has to pay whatever instalments he had missed, even though they amount to more than one half.

There may be an *advantage* in having goods on hire purchase if one unexpectedly gets into financial difficulties. For example when creditors get judgement for large sums of money, they can enforce these judgement debts by instructing the court bailiff to take goods and furniture. *But* the court bailiffs are not allowed to take anything which is held on hire purchase because it belongs to the hire purchase company. In contrast this means that we can keep all hire purchase goods. Credit sales are in fact the customer's property and the bailiffs can take them.

Avoiding

1) If you cannot keep up the instalments, the best course is to write a frank letter to the hire purchase company or telephone them and put your cards on the table. Nothing upsets them so much as your keeping silent and doing nothing.
2) Usually H.P. companies are prepared to accept reduced instalments if they are satisfied that your finances have taken a turn for the worse.

Going to court

If the creditor insists on taking you to court, the judge will usually allow you to keep the goods provided you pay reasonable instalments. You fill in a form supplied by the Court giving a full account of your financial position so the Court can fix what instalments are reasonable. If you pay these instalments regularly into court, you can keep the goods. The form can be sent to the Court by post but always go yourself if you can. If not, send a relative or friend.

WISEGUIDE

Honesty is certainly the best policy when it comes to H.P. if you have difficulties in paying.

Buying second hand cars

Buying second hand goods can be dangerous because they may be subject to a hire purchase agreement. This used to be particularly common with a second hand motor car. If it was on hire purchase the innocent buyer suffered. As the goods in law belong to the hire purchase company, they used to be able to claim them back.

Nowadays however, a private buyer of a car will be able to keep it provided he did not know it was on hire purchase and genuinely believed that the seller was entitled to sell it.

WISEGUIDE

Make sure that whoever sells you goods, actually owns them in the first place.

Defective goods

There is also another advantage in buying under hire purchase because the company cannot get out of liability if the goods are defective or unsuitable. If the same goods are bought on credit sale, the company can state that they are not responsible. Money can be claimed back in these cases, only if there is something very seriously wrong with the goods, for example, if the motor of a washing machine burnt out within a few days.

In one case a motor cycle bought on credit sale had so many *minor* things wrong with it that taken altogether they rendered the machine such a bad buy that the sellers were held liable.

Cancelling agreements

Once you sign a hire purchase agreement on trade premises, i.e. in the shop, you are bound by its terms, even though you did not read it through carefully. The rule is that you cannot welsh on a document you have signed, merely because you did not trouble to read it. Even if you cannot understand English or cannot read, you are still bound by it, *unless you can show that someone had misled you as to its true nature and contents.*

Cancellation is possible when an agreement is not signed in a shop or trade premises, but has been signed, say, at home. In this case there is a second chance to "*re-think*" the transaction but you must *act quickly* – within 4 days.

● As soon as you get the second copy of the agreement through the post, you must write a letter *at once* cancelling the agreement.

Cancellation is possible even if money has been paid; it must then be handed back. If the company or its representative tries to talk you out of cancelling it, the best course is to report the matter at once to the police, or go to see a solicitor.

The Hire Purchase Acts protect anyone buying goods up to £2,000 in value. (So anyone buying a Rolls Royce on hire purchase will not have the benefit of what has been mentioned above.) Under £2,000 the hire purchase company must observe all the regulations laid down by the law. If it breaks a regulation it has no rights under the agreement and cannot claim back the goods. The most important regulation is that the agreement must be in writing. It would also be serious for the company if they failed to send to the hirer, within 7 days, a second copy of any agreement which had been signed by the hirer at his own home.

WISEGUIDE

The purchaser in an H.P. or credit sale agreement has considerable rights. Make sure you know them.

Shopping

When you see goods in a shop window marked at a certain price, it does not mean to say that you can insist on buying them at that price. It is up to the seller to decide whether he wants to sell them. For example he may put in the window a mink coat with a price tag of £20. Unfortunately you cannot go in and

insist on buying it. But the shop could be liable to be fined since 1968 for offering to supply goods with a misleading price tag.

Defects

When you buy goods in a shop for cash, the law does not assume a guarantee except in special circumstances. It is up to the customer to examine the goods carefully and see that they are suitable. If you go into an electrical shop and ask for an electric kettle, the shopkeeper must give you one, which will work. If it blows up in use because it is defective, he must replace it. And if when it blows up, it injures your hand, the maker of the kettle would be liable to pay damages.

Guarantees

This does not apply to any defect which was obvious if you had bothered to inspect the goods. If you buy a pound of fruit and on going home find it unfit to eat, you cannot claim your money back because you could have examined it before you left the shop. By paying your money and taking the goods you lose your rights to complain.

Sometimes defects may not appear until you start to use the article. A suit of clothes may look very well when you first put it on but if all the stitching comes undone within a few days, you are entitled to take it back and demand a replacement.

Relying on the shopkeeper's advice

Generally however, the law does not protect the buyer and so it is up to him to examine the goods carefully and make his mind that they are *what he wants*.

If you ask the shopkeeper to recommend an article, e.g. if you want it for a particular purpose, then the shopkeeper is liable for anything he recommends. For example if you wanted a vacuum cleaner suitable for cleaning a private hotel, i.e. a heavy duty model and he recommended one which was only suitable for light household work, he would be liable since you have relied on his recommendation. He is selling vacuum cleaners and is expected to know something about them.

Misleading labels and advertisements

Since 1968 it is a criminal offence for a shopkeeper to describe goods in a misleading way. Any statement made about the goods must be literally true. If he describes a tablecloth as "pure Irish linen", he would be guilty of an offence if it turns out to contain a certain percentage of artificial fibre. Also the buyer would be entitled to his money back.

WISEGUIDE

There is some protection for the customer under the law, but it is not complete. There is no substitute for careful inspection of goods before you leave the shop. If in doubt, insist that the shopkeeper writes on the bill that he guarantees them.

Price reductions

It is now an offence if the shopkeeper misleads customers into thinking that goods have been reduced in price. A shop can only show price reductions if in fact the goods have previously been sold there at the higher price for a reasonable period and this is a genuine reduction. The shop is allowed however, to mark down the article from the manufacturer's "recommended price" if in fact this is true.

The false statement does not have to be in writing. If the shop assistant assures you that the tablecloth is pure linen, then that is sufficient to render the shopkeeper liable if it is not.

WISEGUIDE

The Act does not *entitle* you to compensation but only punishes the shopkeeper. If after being prosecuted the shopkeeper still refuses to pay the compensation, you should take the matter up with a solicitor.

The Moneylenders Acts

These Acts regulate very strictly the amount of interest which a moneylender may charge.

Going to a moneylender (see chapter 3) is obviously a last resort and so from the moneylender's point of view the borrower is seldom a very good risk. To compensate for the high risk involved, the real interest rates are correspondingly high, often up to 48% a year. On a short-term borrowing, this may not be excessive. For example, if we need £100 desperately but only for 6 months, the interest charges will be £24. In certain circumstances you may well think that this is worthwhile in order to get the £100 when you need it.

The law is very careful to see that the moneylender does not exploit a needy borrower.

Even after borrowing the money and signing the agreement, the borrower is entitled to complain to the court that the rate of interest charged is too high. If it exceeds 48% a year, the judge is *bound* to assume that it is excessive and he may reduce it to such amount as he thinks reasonable in the circumstances.

In one case, a woman borrowed money at the rate of 80% but the judge was sympathetic towards her because he was satisfied that she lacked business experience and the moneylender had taken advantage of this. The judge therefore reduced the rate of interest payable to 25% a year.

On the other hand, these days a judge would not be sympathetic to a borrower who was merely being extravagant and living beyond his means.

The borrower cannot always assume that the judge will be on his side. In recent cases, rates of interest as high as 120% a year, (=£10 a month for a £100) have been upheld when the borrower was not pressed by necessity but knew perfectly well what he was doing and wished merely to live on an extravagant scale.

Again, if the risk involved *justifies* a high rate of interest the judge would allow it. In one case a loan to a business man at the rate of 80% was allowed because the loan was for a highly profitable and speculative enterprise.

Don't use moneylenders if you can avoid them. Borrowers are protected to some extent by law, but the judge looks at each case on its merits.

The Moneylenders Acts greatly restrict moneylending. If you make a habit of lending money and it becomes a *business* side-line, you may be subject to the Moneylenders Acts if you charge a profitable rate of interest.

   This does not of course apply to making *occasional* loans to friends or relatives.

Restrictions on moneylenders

A moneylender must have a special licence

Points to watch

1) If a court decides that you have been lending money as a business and are not licensed as a moneylender, you cannot claim back the money you have lent. Moreover you may even be held guilty of a criminal offence for not obtaining a Licence from the local Magistrates' Court.

2) A moneylender is subject to severe advertising restrictions. He may not send out circular letters or canvass customers, but he may put a limited form of advertisement in a newspaper.

3) All agreements for lending money *must be in writing* and signed by the borrower. If there is an important error in them it could make the whole transaction invalid and the moneylender would not be able to recover the loan.

4) Anyone borrowing from a moneylender is in a specially privileged position. If he defaults in payment, the lender must take Court action within 12 months of the last payment due. If the moneylender does not take Court action, he loses his right to sue unless the borrower signs a letter acknowledging the debt. In this case the time limit runs for a further 12 months from the date of the letter.

5) Although a moneylender may charge a high rate of interest (up to 48% per annum) he can charge only *simple* interest. He is *not* allowed to charge *compound* interest under any circumstances.

6) Sometimes the moneylending contract contains penalty clauses viz: if an instalment is not paid on time, the borrower must pay interest on that instalment. This is permissible but the rate of interest cannot go above the rate charged for the loan itself, eg if we are paying 20% on the loan, we cannot be made to pay more than 20% on instalments in arrear.

If you have borrowed from a moneylender, make sure that there is a contract and that it is a legal one.

The Law

How to "tie up" your money: settlements and trusts

A settlement is a document by which we can place money, shares or investments in the hands of trustees for the benefit of our wife, children or other dependants.

The trustees are obliged to look after the assets and pay the income in accordance with our wishes as stated in the settlement.

Usually settlements come into effect on death, as the result of a Will, but there are advantages in making a settlement which will begin at once while we are still alive. We can then actually see the Trust working and that our wishes are being carried out before we die.

The object of making a settlement may be to save death duties. Read chapter 15 carefully.

Discretionary trusts

You do not have to give each beneficiary a specific amount of income. You can if you like leave it to the discretion of the Trustees to pay money to those of your dependants who need it. The advantage of this is that if a dependant goes bankrupt, his creditors cannot claim a share of the Trust income because he is not paid it as of right but only at the choice of the Trustees.

This can also protect a beneficiary from his own extravagance. You can specifically state in the Trust that if he goes bankrupt he is not to be paid any more money.

Breaking a trust

It is clear therefore that from the family's point of view, a Trust is not always satisfactory. They may want to get their hands on the capital of the Trust. If all the beneficiaries agree, the Trust can be terminated and the assets divided up. If some of the beneficiaries are under 18, the leave of the Court is required to put an end to the Trust.

Infants and money

In law an infant means *any* person under 18. Since 1969 a person attains his majority on the day of his 18th birthday. Under this age the law protects him.

Limitations on infants

1) An infant cannot legally be made to repay a debt or even pay for goods. He can only be made to pay for such things as food and clothes needed for his personal use.

2) An infant cannot own land or buildings. If one wished to give an infant a house for example, a trust would have to be set up in his favour. In that case the house would be held by Trustees for his benefit.

3) An infant can however own other assets such as money and shares and furniture, i.e. anything except land, and can buy and sell these as he wishes. If he enters into a hire purchase agreement or a credit agreement, he is not bound by it unless

he wants to keep the goods. If he happens to be an infant business genius he may go into business and make contracts. He is not bound by these contracts although they *do* bind the persons with whom he makes them. This sounds unfair and it is best to avoid doing business with a person under 18.

4) Although in law regarded as an infant, he is entitled to hold shares in a company. If he is called on to pay any balance owing on the shares he has a choice. If he wishes to keep the shares he must make the payment asked, but if he considers the shares are valueless he can reject any interest in them. Once he becomes 18, he must make up his mind whether to keep the shares or not. His failure to reject them *then* would mean that in future he was bound to pay any balance owed when called upon.

If someone under 18 does business of any kind, the other party to the contract is bound by what is agreed.

WISEGUIDE

● When a person borrows money, gets a new job or takes on some new responsibility such as the lease of a shop you may be asked to give him a reference. So long as you give the reference honestly and state the facts as known, you are not liable if he defaults.

● You would be liable only if you carelessly stated facts about his financial position without checking that they were accurate.

● You are obliged to state what you know to be true, even though for example it may prevent an ex-employee from getting a new job or may persuade the shop owner not to grant him a lease. Even if this results in his losing the job or the shop, he cannot claim damages from you for libel provided you honestly believed when you gave the reference that you were telling the truth.

Liability when giving a reference

Points to watch

In certain respects the law concerning money in Scotland and Northern Ireland differs from that in England and Wales. Check the position if you live in these areas, or are involved in financial dealings in them. Talk to your solicitor before making a will. But for most people the differences show up in the buying and selling of houses:

For instance Scots:
● Tend to buy and sell houses and flats through solicitors rather than estate agents
● Have different laws governing purchase and sale arrangements
● Borrow their mortgage money on different terms
● Own their homes under different laws.

The Northern Irish:
● Generally live in leasehold rather than freehold properties

Law in Scotland and Northern Ireland

● Generally pay an estate agent's commission when they buy instead of when they sell a home.

Solicitors and Estate Agents Though there are estate agents in the larger cities and towns, most Scottish property deals are handled by solicitors acting as 'property agents'.

Contracts Instead of buying and selling homes 'subject to contract' as in the rest of the United Kingdom, the Scots make a written offer stating the price they are prepared to pay.

This offer is made subject to good title being provided and the buyer being assured entry on a specific date, and becomes legally binding on both sides once accepted in writing by the seller.

This means that you must be specially careful about everything you put on paper.

Of course there is nothing to prevent you telephoning the seller or his solicitor and making a verbal offer, just as there is nothing to prevent a seller collecting written offers and then selecting the highest.

The system also means that once a seller has accepted your offer in writing he cannot then change his mind if a better bid arrives. But do be careful.

Mortgages Mortgage arrangements are different as well.

Feu Duty Nearly all Scottish property is owned under a system of feudal tenure dating back to the Middle Ages.

In practice this means that the property belongs to a feudal landlord or *superior* for ever and ever. The buyer purchases the equivalent of a perpetual lease, and pays a small perpetual ground rent or *Feu Duty*.

The system can have certain advantages. For instance feudal tenure makes for a much clearer relationship between superior and tenant when buying into a property split into a number of units.

But there are also some hidden snags. For instance you may find that your superior has the right to control what you do with your home.

However the system may change if reforms proposed by a recent government commission become law. These reforms recommended that tenants be given the right to compulsorily purchase their tenancy, much as certain leaseholders were given the right to purchase their leaseholds in England and Wales under the Leasehold Reform Act.

Northern Ireland Leaseholds Nearly all property in Northern Ireland is owned on a leasehold rather than freehold basis.

For all practical purposes this may make little difference in buying and selling a home, for leases generally extend over as long as 999 years or even longer.

But the buyer should take care to know how long he or his descendants could own their house or flat.

Commissions Although the Northern Irish buy and sell homes according to the same laws as in England and Wales, the buyer normally pays the estate agent's commission.

Index

208